JANUA LINGUARUM

STUDIA MEMORIAE
NICOLAI VAN WIJK DEDICATA

edenda curat

C. H. VAN SCHOONEVELD

Indiana University

Series Practica, 104

ARTICLE AND NOUN
IN ENGLISH

by

JOHN HEWSON

Memorial University of Newfoundland

1972

MOUTON

THE HAGUE · PARIS

LIBRARY OF CONGRESS CATALOG CARD NUMBER: 70—173385

Printed in Hungary

FOREWORD

The seemingly impenetrable mysteries of human language have afforded an object of curiosity and study for centuries. Every age has had its own point of view, its own philosophy, its own attitudes to language. These attitudes vary from those that hold all language to be based on a universal grammar to those that regard language as nothing more than a capricious accumulation of sounds. The Greeks were the first Europeans to attempt linguistic analysis; successive generations have followed in their footsteps: Latin grammar was based on the Greek model and it in turn formed the basis of the grammars of the modern vernaculars.

Grammar then became normative or prescriptive, insisting on the Latin model; atrocities are perpetrated even today upon the grammar of English because the traditional model has been the Latin one: we are taught that *O table!* is the vocative case; that *It is I* is correct, even if in French, a direct descendant of Latin, one says *C'est moi.*

In the nineteenth century, because of comparative Indo-European studies, men became aware of the historical evolution of languages, and the study of phonetics, especially historical phonetics, grew apace. In our own century phoneticians have analysed the sounds of human language and the means of producing them sufficiently well to be able to construct machines capable of synthesizing such sounds. At the same time, interest developed in the subject of phonology (phonemics) or the systemic categorization that lies behind the phonetic fact.

There has also been a continuing evolution in grammatical studies, even if these latter have had but little effect on the schools. Sweet had many interesting insights on the grammatical structure of English, and Jespersen's comments and analyses frequently achieve profundity. They represent a tradition that is in danger of being overlooked; modern linguistic scholarship, where it treads new paths, must not forget, in its enthusiasm for the new, the relevant scholarship of the past. Linguistics, as a discipline, is not new; it has a long history, and the neglect of great scholars of the past may result in the neglect of a valuable chain of enquiry or in puzzlement over problems that had, in fact, long been settled.

In recent years, linguistic research has devoted a great deal of energy to
what has come to be known as transformational grammar. Growing out of the
ideas of symbolic logic, mathematics and cybernetics, transformational grammars view language implicitly, if not always explicitly, as a dynamism: they
are concerned with stating the grammatical fact in dynamic terms, a principle
which is a major step forward.

Transformational grammars, however, have certain limits: they aim to state
and to describe, not to explain. The goal of the present study is to go beyond
the statement of competence and to investigate, in one small area, the mental
mechanism, the system, that lies behind the syntactic fact.

As a point of departure, this study utilizes the linguistic theories of Gustave
Guillaume, and may be considered as a justification and elaboration of his
ideas. At his death in 1960 Guillaume left a small body of published materials,
not at all easy to follow or understand (for which reason it has been very
largely ignored or completely misunderstood), a vast amount of unpublished
material, and an oral tradition among his immediate disciples. I have been in
the fortunate position of being able to draw upon all three sources.

In Chapter I the relevant historical facts concerning the use of the article
are presented and examined: some may wonder at the introduction of the
historical element, but the reason for this state of affairs is quite simple. The
functioning of a particular system must be explained in synchronic terms, but
the development of the system itself is a matter of history; to understand a
system fully, one must look at it from both perspectives. There are in fact two
different processes, both interrelated and interconnected; the generative operations that produce *parole* and result in a phrase or a sentence (synchronic)
and the generative development of *langue* that produces what Saussure called
an *état de langue* (diachronic).

Chapter II presents Guillaume's view of language with a discussion of
method. This sketch is necessarily brief, and is intended as an introduction to
the theoretical chapters, not as an exhaustive survey of Guillaume's ideas and
their place in modern linguistic thought. Chapter III is an attempt to delineate
a theory of the substantive, using the psychomechanics of Guillaume as a
point of departure, and Chapter IV presents the English article system as seen
from the point of view of Guillaume's theory. The remaining three chapters
investigate the relevance of the theoretical proposals to the three types of
article usage: indefinite, definite, and zero.

The psychomechanics of Guillaume is based on an Einsteinian *Weltan-
schauung* and is therefore difficult to grasp on first encounter: it is necessary
to gain a broad insight into the whole before all the parts can be seen to fit
thoroughly into place. It is, however, for explanatory purposes, an extra-
ordinarily powerful theory: without it, this work would have been little more
than a compilation of puzzling facts. If puzzles remain they must be attri-

buted to the inadequacies of the author, to the novelty of the exercise, and the
abstruseness of the matter; the work is therefore offered as an essay in the
purest sense of the term.

This book has been published with the help of a grant from the Human-
ities Research Council of Canada, using funds provided by the Canada
Council. I would like to express my gratitude to both these bodies, and also
to the many people who helped me in various ways, especially Roch Valin,
Walter Hirtle and André Joly.

St. John's, Newfoundland
August 1969   *John Hewson*

TABLE OF CONTENTS

I

INTRODUCTION: THE HISTORICAL ASPECT OF THE ARTICLE

A. INDO-EUROPEAN

The article is, in the Indo-European languages that possess it, a systemic development: Indo-European had no article, and there is documentary evidence in some of these languages of the origins as well as the development of an article system.[1] We can trace the definite articles of Greek and the Romance vernaculars back to their origins in an ancient demonstrative, and the Germanic languages yield evidence of the evolution of their article systems from the crude but mutually similar systems found in the earliest texts.

It is a fact that languages, whereas they frequently borrow great numbers of lexical items from each other, rarely if ever borrow grammatical systems. This alone should deter us from believing that the article systems of the Indo-European languages spring from a common fount in Classical Greek. Statements supporting this point of view must, therefore, be examined carefully and the evidence weighed with some deliberation. Bonfante states:

Homeric Greek had no real article; the definite article is therefore a conquest of classical Greek (the indefinite article arrives even later).

Classical Latin had no article either, but spoken Latin certainly had it in the imperial period, and from there it spread to all the Romance and the modern Germanic languages (though Gothic still lacked it). There is no question, therefore, that the article spread from Greece (hence its presence in Bulgarian), and that it is in Europe, at least, a gift of Greek culture; but it is also obvious that it was adopted by the other languages because it was felt as a precious and useful enrichment at a certain stage of cultural development.[2]

Such evidence as exists not only does not corroborate the statements made in this passage, but leads to a rebuttal of them:

[1] Cf. W. Hodler, *Grundzüge einer germanischen Artikellehre* (Heidelberg, 1954), p. 9: "Wir dürfen also wohl mit Sicherheit annehmen, dass der Artikel der indogermanischen Ursprache gefehlt hat, und dass der indische, der griechische (gemeingriechische), der germanische und später der romanische Artikel in den Einzelsprachen entwickelt worden sind."

[2] G. U. Bonfante, "Semantics in Linguistics", in: *Encyclopaedia Britannica* (1958 ed.) Vol 20, p. 313G.

(i) There is no evidence of an article in spoken Latin of the imperial period. Taking the most chatty and conversational of texts of the early fifth century A.D., the *Peregrinatio ad Loca Sancta*,[3] narrative of a journey made in 415—418, we find (although there is an increased frequency in the use of demonstratives, foreshadowing the genesis of an article system) (a) many nouns lacking determiners and (b) the equal use of *hic, iste, ipse* and *ille*. These characteristics suggest that such a system had not yet appeared:

Nam *haec aqua* tam grandis et tam pura, quam videtis in *isto loco*, de *ipso fonte* venit. Tunc ergo gratias ei agere coepi et rogare, ut duceret nos ad *locum*.[4]

(ii) There is no evidence that the article spread from Romance to Germanic. The documents we have suggest that, if anything, the reverse could be true. The Strasbourg Oaths of 842 A.D. between Charles the Bald and Louis the German contain what is considered to be the first text in French (the oath of Charles), followed by its equivalent (the oath of Louis) in Rhineland Franconian *(i.e.* Old High German) with simply a substitution of the name Charles for Louis. The German text uses an article; the French none. Compare the following extracts:

(a) Pro deo amour et pro christian poblo
    In godes minna ind in *thes* christanes folches
(b) Si (Lodhuigs) sagrament, que ... iurat ...
    Oba (Karl) *then* eid, then er ... gesuor, ...

Nor are these forms demonstratives, which are also to be found with their Germanic *s* stem:

(a) d'*ist* di in avant
    fon *thesemo* dage frammordes
(b) *cist* meon fradre
    thesan minan bruodher

(iii) The statement that Gothic lacked an article is supported by some scholars in the field (notably Streitberg: *Gotisches Elementarbuch*, pp. 185—6)[5] but the work of Sauvageot[6] painstakingly demonstrates that Gothic had an article system, although a very rudimentary one, and that it corresponds to the systems of early Old High German, Old Norse and Old English. Since Wulfila (d. 383) who translated the gospels into Gothic from the Greek was a contemporary of St. Jerome (*c.* 340—420), it becomes revealing to compare

---

[3] *Silviae vel potius Aetheriae Peregrinatio ad Loca Sancta*, ed. E. Heraeus (Heidelberg 1908, 4th ed. 1939).
[4] From a passage quoted by W. D. Elcock, *The Romance Languages* (London, 1960).
[5] See also footnote 26 of this chapter.
[6] A. Sauvageot, *L'emploi de l'article en gotique* (Paris, 1929).

the Gothic version with the Vulgate gospels; and with the other old Germanic texts:[7]

(a) Gothic   gaswalt þan jah *sa gabeiga*
       Vulgate   mortuus est autem *dives*
       OHG   Astarp ouch *ther ôtago*
       Norse   þo do ok *inn auđgi*
(b) Gothic   und *pana* þridjan dag
       Vulgate   in diem tertium
       OHG   unzan *then* thriton tag

Sauvageot also rejects the suggestion that the Gothic article is a simple *calque* on the Greek original on the following grounds: (1) There is too close a correspondence between the usage in Gothic and that of the other ancient Germanic texts, (2) the other Germanic texts are based on the Vulgate which had no article, (3) the Gothic usage is quite different from the Greek.[8]

(iv) If the Greek article affected Bulgarian, it would be difficult to explain why Slovene and Serbo-Croat, related languages which might also have been influenced by Greek, have no article. Since the Bulgarian article is postposed, it is a doubtful imitation of the Greek, which always precedes the noun.[9]

(v) If it were obvious that the article "was adopted by the other languages because it was felt as a precious and useful enrichment at a certain stage of cultural development", it can be assumed that other linguistic communities which had attained a degree of cultural sophistication equal to that of the Greeks of the classical era or even of the pre-Norman invasion Anglo-Saxons would have sought to develop an article system. It is incredible, therefore, that

---

[7] Examples based on Sauvageot, pp. 62—63 (Luke 16: 22) and p. 60 (Matt. 27: 64).
[8] Hodler, *op. cit.*, p. 11, with marked irony comments on those scholars who seek for too easy an explanation of the use of the article in the texts of early Germanic: "Die Weglassung des Artikels aber wird von Mourek und Jäger gern durch den Einfluss der lateinischen Vorlage erklärt, wie umgekehrt die griechische Vorlage von manchen Forschern zu sehr für die Artikelsetzung bei Wulfila verantwortlich gemacht wird." The contentions that similar usage is unusually frequent (because of a Greek model), or unusually infrequent (because of a Latin model) show (a) scholarly failing to face fact and (b) explanations that are not only linguistically dubious but also self-contradictory.
[9] Still others regard the postposeted article of Bulgarian (and Rumanian) as a loan from Albanian. See Paul Christophersen, *The Articles* (Copenhagen and London, 1939), p. 18. If such be the case, what is the origin of the postposed article of North Germanic? Hodler, *op. cit.*, p. 9, justly and sensibly remarks, "Für den Artikel ist es nicht wesentlich, ob er vor dem Substantiv stehe oder hinter demselben". Guillaume comments *(Le Problème de l'article* [Paris, 1919], p. 17): "L'explication de ce fait déborde la théorie spéciale de l'article. Il s'agit d'une survivance de l'ancien ordre de mots indo-européen qui voulait que le mot grammatical fît suite au mot lexicographique. Au surplus, la postposition de l'article est spéciale au groupe oriental, et ceci semble démontrer qu'elle est la conséquence d'un certain état de langue. Accessoirement, on peut y voir un moyen de fortifier l'opposition entre le démonstratif anaphorique et le démonstratif direct, dans le cas où celui-ci reste préposé."

the grandeur of Rome should have passed into the history books without the language of the empire having developed an article.[10]

The facts that (1) languages frequently borrow vocabulary and rarely if ever grammatical systems, and (2) geographically separated languages (e.g. Greek-Armenian[11]) — as also different types of language (Greek-Arabic) — develop articles independently the one of the other, suggest that the article system satisfies a practical need that arises in the evolution of a language.

This practical need is for a morpheme to counteract the drift, within the system of the noun, towards a greater generalization. This drift is historically attested, in the Indo-European languages, in the disappearance of cases, indeed of whole declensions, concomitant with the development of a greater range of abstract expression. Guillaume had already perceived in 1919 that:

Les divers systèmes d'articles n'ont d'autre but que de pratiquer, avec plus ou moins d'élégance, ces 'coupures' dans le nom total.

Twenty years later, in the first volume of *Acta Linguistica*,[12] he was to propose an underlying reason for this twofold development of the decay of declension systems and the appearance of article systems: the gradual drift, over the centuries, towards an ever earlier interpenetration of the particularizing notional ideation by the generalizing structural ideation.[13]

The historical facts, indeed, show a correlation between the appearance of article systems and the reduction of the eight-case system of Indo-European. Those languages that have preserved this case system most faithfully (Lithuanian, Russian, etc.) are precisely those that have developed no article system. It is notable that Classical Greek, having, like Germanic, only four important cases and three declensions, had reached a simpler stage of noun declension than that to be found in Classical Latin and had a far greater range of abstract expression: the student learning to imitate Classical Latin models has to refrain from beginning periods with abstract nouns and has to be careful to write *vir probus* for a *man of honour;* one cannot help thinking of the despair of Cicero at the rendering of philosophy in the Latin language. Whereas, on the other hand, the Latin noun had a system of five working cases, the modern French noun has normally only a single phonetic form, and this serves for both singular and plural. The phonetic form [*pje*] for example, is all that is

---

[10]   The facts of Classical Latin and modern Russian speak for themselves.

[11]   *Cf.* Meillet, *Introduction à l'étude comparative des langues indo-européennes* (Paris, 8th ed., 1937): "L'arménien qui a un article différent à tous égards de l'article grec ou de l'article des langues romanes, a dès ses premiers textes des groupes nominaux liés et a tendu à faire ses phrases à l'aide de groupes de mots rigides avec un ordre de mots de plus en plus fixe." The first texts date from the fifth century A.D.

[12]   The article, entitled "Esquisse d'une théorie psychologique de la déclinaison" is reprinted in *Langage et science du langage*.

[13]   For an elucidation of these terms see below, pp. 63—67.

left of the total declension of the Latin noun *pes, pedis*. This reduction has been accompanied by a continuing tendency for the significate of the bare unqualified noun, which in Latin was closely attached to concrete senses, to evolve to a state of pure notion where it reflects only the abstract sense,[14] and equally by a continued evolution of the article system, which, in Modern French, has undergone very great evolutive development.[15]

B. GERMANIC

The article itself evolves from a demonstrative pronoun which also undergoes weakening of its demonstrative force in becoming an article.[16] Henry relates the early history of the English definite article:[17]

La majeure partie de la déclinaison de l'article défini est empruntée à un démonstratif indo-européen *so *to ... En sanscrit, en grec homérique et jusqu'en latin, ce démonstratif a gardé toute sa valeur et signifie 'ce, celui'; mais en grec classique déjà, il est devenu simple article, se traduit uniment par 'le' et précède obligatoirement le substantif. L'histoire des langues germaniques nous fait assister à une évolution toute semblable: le même thème, qui est exclusivement démonstratif, avec valeur un tant soit peu affaiblie, en gotique, en anglo-saxon et en vieil-allemand, est aujourd'hui article d'un emploi à peu près constant et obligatoire en allemand, obligatoire dans la majorité des cas en anglais. La transition est bien aisée à concevoir: quand nous lisons dans Ulfilas '*manne sums aihta twans sununs, jah qaþ sa juhiza ize du attin*,' 'des hommes un certain avait deux fils, et dit *celui* plus jeune d'eux à père', ou en anglo-saxon: '*soðlice ut eode se sædere hys sæd to sawenne*', 'véritablement hors alla ce semeur sa semence pour semer', nous traduisons[18] sans hésitation 'le cadet dit ... le semeur sortit ...'; et en fait le démonstratif est déjà un article.

It is doubtful whether Proto-Germanic possessed an article,[19] in spite of the unity of system apparent in the earliest Germanic texts, because of the different forms employed by the different groups and because of the postposed article to be found in North Germanic:

---

[14] See Guillaume, *Le Problème*, pp. 68—87.
[15] See Guillaume, *Le Problème*, pp. 23—24 and 89—94.
[16] "In allen indogermanischen Sprachen tritt diese Schwächung der Deixis bei den Pronomina mehr oder weniger stark auf, aber immer macht sich auch das Bestreben bemerkbar, den Verlust an Deixiskraft durch Bildung neuer Pronomina oder durch Verstärkung der alten Wieder wettzumachen." H. M. Heinrichs, *Studien zum bestimmten Artikel in den germanischen Sprachen* (Giessen, 1954), p. 17.
[17] V. Henry, *Précis de grammaire comparée de l'anglais et de l'allemand* (Paris, 1906), pp. 232—3.
[18] It should be pointed out, however, that it is dangerous to base judgements on the result of translation into target languages.
[19] *Cf.* Hodler, *op. cit.*, p. 9: "Die Entwicklung scheint ... einzelsprachlich gewesen zu sein".

Gothic	sa, so, þata
Norse	enn, en, et
OHG	der, diu, daz
OE	se, seo, þæt

Another factor suggesting that Proto-Germanic possessed no article is that in the earliest texts — Gothic — the article is very little removed from its demonstrative sense although the usage represents a stage well removed from the breakup of Germanic unity, according to the evidence of the other dialects, even if their texts be from a later period.

It appears, then, that Indo-European had no article and that the article systems do not appear in the Germanic family until after the breakup of Germanic unity. Furthermore the appearance of article systems at different moments of history in different languages and in different types of language supports the contention that article systems are not borrowed, but represent the exploiting of native resources to meet a need arising at a particular moment in the development of a language.

C. OLD AND MIDDLE ENGLISH
1. *Definite article*

The Old English article, forerunner of the Modern English, shows a more advanced stage of development than the article in Wulfila's gospels, due no doubt to the four further centuries of evolution before the appearance of the first Old English documents. It had a full declension, similar to the Classical Greek or Modern German:

	Singular			Plural
	M.	F.	N.	
Nom.	se	seo	þæt	þa
Acc.	þone	þa	þæt	þa
Gen.	þæs	þære	þæs	þara
Dat.	þæm	þære	þæm	þæm

and the remains of an instrumental: þy, þon.

In the early tenth century the neutralization of unstressed vowels in English, which had developed in the North, became generalized throughout the country. Since the various forms of the article and the final syllables of nouns were commonly unstressed, this contributed largely to a reduction of the forms of the article and to the disappearance of inflection in the noun during the Middle English period.[20] By the end of the thirteenth century the modern form *the* is

---

[20]   It must be realized however that this is not the sole reason for the disappearance of the morphology of the noun and the article: case was disappearing not only as a phonetic element, but also as a mental, grammatical category. (See Guillaume, *Langage et science du langage*, p. 107.)

the only one to be found except where a final consonant lived on for a while by way of a liaison:

> A Cook they hadde with hem for the nones[21] (= for the (n) once)
> the tone of seynte Katryne and the tother of seynt George[22]
> (= the (t) one ... the (t) other)

Meanwhile the neuter stressed *þæt* and its plural *þa* go on to become genuine demonstratives, to the latter being added an *s*. It is of interest to note that *this* and *these* are, like the indefinite article, introductory in sense; *that* and *those* are not only closely related etymologically to the definite article, but also reflect its referential force.[23]

2. *Indefinite article*

There would seem to be no indefinite article in early Old English:[24]

(a) þæt dyde unhold mann
an enemy did that

(b) swa swa wulf
like a wolf

(c) ic wat þæt þu eart heard mann
I know that thou art a hard man

The numeral *an*, however, had already developed the sense of *a certain* on its way to becoming an indefinite article.[25] It was declined as an adjective:

	M.	F.	N.
Nom.	an	an	an
Acc.	anne	ane	an
Gen.	anes	anre	anes
Dat.	anum	anre	anum

It can also be found in a weak declension with the meaning *alone*. The stressed form gives the Modern English numeral *one;* the unstressed form suffers the same phonetic attrition as the definite article during late Old English and the

---

[21] Chaucer, CT B Mil 1159, qu. T. F. Mustanoja, *A Middle English Syntax*, Part I (Helsinki, 1960), p. 233.

[22] Fifty Wills, 117, qu. Mustanoja, *A Middle English Syntax*, p. 233.

[23] The evidence on which this comment is based must necessarily come later. See pp. 82—84.

[24] Examples taken from Davis, *Sweet's Anglo-Saxon Primer* (OUP, 9th. ed., 1953) p. 49. These citations are from early West Saxon documents.

[25] It is sometimes exceptionally difficult to say what is an article and what is not (see below, footnote 26), but when the usage is very rare, it is safer to suppose the use of a proto-article, as here.

Middle English periods and can be found in Chaucer as *a* (before a consonant) and *an* (before a vowel or *h*); prior to this there is a certain confusion of forms:

> *An* hule and *one* nigtingale (Owl and Nightingale, 4)

D. DEVELOPMENT OF ARTICLE SYSTEM

1. *Definite article*

In use the Old English definite article seems to speakers of Modern English more like a mixture of demonstrative and article;[26] some usages would be translated by a modern article:

> þa endleoftan tid = the eleventh hour

others by a demonstrative:

> þa arison ealle þa fæmnan . . .
> Then all those women arose . . . (Matt 15: 7)
> (Translation of Revised Rheims-Douay version)

still others by either an article or a demonstrative:

> Soðlice þæt cild weox and was gestrangod
> And the/that child grew and became strong (Luke 2: 40)

This is to be expected. Systems evolve historically and the shift from the original demonstrative to the modern article is evolutive and not immediate. Likewise, the noun system develops but slowly as it shakes itself loose from gender and case and expands its extensivity or horizon of abstraction.[27]

The historical evidence of this twofold evolution is not lacking. In Old English many types of noun, and certain types of usage, show resistance to an article that has traces of demonstrative force. The bare unqualified noun still retains enough of its basic concrete senses to be used in many prepositional phrases without an article, even where the article would now be obligatory. *e.g.*[28]

> (i) (a) of frymðe = from the beginning
>   (b) on sæ = in the sea

---

[26] The same is true of the articles in all the early Germanic texts. It was the fact that the usage in Gotihic was so close to that of the demonstrative that caused Streitberg (see above page 12) to deny that Gothic had an article. His manner of making this assertion reveals that his experience of the article in more evolved vernaculars may well have influenced his opinion: "Versteht man unter 'Artikel' das gewohnheitsmässig und obligatorisch zugefügte Demonstrativum, das eine Person oder Sache als bekannt charakterisiert, so hat das Gotische keinen Artikel."

[27] The significance of this point will be developed in Chapters III and IV.

[28] Examples taken from Grammar and Text of *Sweet's Primer*.

Proper nouns that carry some degree of generality also resist the use of the article in Old English, for example the names of nations:

(ii) (a) Bretta cyning = the Britons' king
      (b) hie feohtan ongean Peohtas = they fight against the Picts

as also the names of rivers:

(iii) (a) up on Sigene = up into the Seine
       (b) ofer Temese = over the Thames

These instances, however, represent no rigid rules: stylistic and contextual influences, such as an immediate anaphoric reference may cause the article to be used, as in the only known case of an article used with a river name in Old English:

Weonodland wæs us ealne weg on steorbord oþ Wislemuðan. *Seo Wisle* is swyðe mycel ea.[29]

By Middle English times usages (i) and (ii) usually required an article:

(i)   (a) in þe bygynning God made . . .[30]
      (b) But in the sea she dryveth forth her weye[31]
(ii) (a) And namely the Thebans ofte sythe[32]
      (b) Again the Scottes, as men may wel here[33]

but considerations of versification do not prevent the occasional use of a nation without the article:

Whan this Calkas knew . . .
That *Grekes* sholden swich a peple bringe[34]

Rare however is the use of an article in Middle English with the names of rivers:

To fisshe in Tybre, whan him liste pleye[35]

although in Late Middle English prose the usage begins to occur with the names of foreign rivers:

wiþ þe Reyne in þe norþ side, wiþ þe Rone in þe est[36]

[29] Alfred, Oros. 20, qu. Mustanoja, *Middle English Syntax*, p. 242.
[30] Trevisa's Dialogus (London, OUP, 1925), p. 95.
[31] Chaucer CT B ML 875.
[32] Chaucer CT A KL 1877.
[33] Chaucer CT B ML 580.
[34] Chaucer TC I 73.
[35] Chaucer CT B MK 3666.
[36] Trev. Higd. I. 271, qu. Mustanoja, *op. cit.*, p. 243.

This use of the article is still rare in Early Modern English:

   (i)   His private arbours, and new planted orchards
         On this side Tiber[37]
  (ii) Upon the caves of Nile[38]
 (iii) 'Twixt Elbe and Sala[39]
 (iv) Come, you shall have Trent turned[40]
  (v) And were baptized of him in Jordan[41]
 (vi) Are not Abana and Pharpar, rivers of Damascus, better[42]
(vii) Go and wash in Jordan seven times[43]

These last examples are from the late sixteenth and early seventeenth centuries. By the middle of the seventeenth century the modern usage is to be found:

and all over the Thames, with one's faces in the wind, you were almost burned by a shower of fire drops[44]

The fact that it was the names of foreign rivers that first developed the use of the article has led some scholars to believe that the final establishment of the article with English river names is due to French and German influence.[45] This is not necessarily so; that which is close and known keeps more easily its status as a full proper noun. In Modern English the article is used with foreign buildings, *e.g. the Mariinsky Palace*, but if, one day, we add an article before *Buckingham Palace*, it certainly will not be under the influence of Russian. And if the usage did come into English from French and German influence, one may ask under what influence did French and German develop the usage? It seems more reasonable to regard the parallel developments in French, German and English as examples of a common and similar movement: all nouns that have a one-to-one relationship with a real object tend to resist the use of the article; this resistance is stronger when the object has clearly defined outlines, weaker when the outlines are vague.[46] Hence names of nations will normally develop an article before the names of rivers; the names of individual people will resist the use of the article till the last. It also follows that names of foreign items show less resistance to usage with an article than do names of familiar objects.

[37]   Shakespeare, *Julius Caesar*, I. i. 49.
[38]   Shakespeare, *Antony and Cleopatra*, V. ii. 354.
[39]   Shakespeare, *Henry the Fifth*, I. ii. 52.
[40]   Shakespeare, *Henry the Fourth*, Part One, III. i. 135.
[41]   *King James Bible*, Matthew 3: 6.
[42]   *King James Bible*, II Kings 5: 12.
[43]   *King James Bible*, II Kings 5: 10.
[44]   Pepys' Diary, description of the Great Fire of 1666.
[45]   See Mustanoja, *Middle English Syntax*, p. 243.
[46]   See below, p. 109.

2. *The indefinite article*

We have seen that the numeral *an* was sometimes used in early Old English with the sense of *a certain*. It is during the Old English period that this numeral begins to develop into an article. In the West Saxon gospels of the end of the tenth century we may find instances similar to the modern usage:

> OE: bringað an fatt stierc and ofsleað
> Latin: adducite vitulum saginatum, et occidite   (Luke 15: 23)
> OE: se Hæland astah on ænne munt
> Latin: subiit in montem Jesus   (John 6: 3)

That the indefinite article was a secondary development, however, is also evident from the fact that *sum* (which gives Modern English *some*) is also used for individualizing indirect reference. In other words, there is no binary contrast of definite and indefinite, as in Modern English, but a contrast of definite and zero on the one hand, and on the other a contrast of *an* and *sum* for specific individualizing reference.[47] By the twelfth century, however, *an* is rapidly taking over the uses of *sum* and at the same time losing its inflections and becoming frequently reduced to short, unstressed *an*.[48] P. Süsskand's comparison of some of the Lambeth Homilies[49] has revealed that the copyist came across two cases of *sum* and replaced them by *an;* he found five cases of *an*, kept all, and added three more where previously there had been none — all three reflecting the modern usage. By the end of the fourteenth century we find the indefinite article used in Chaucer much as in Modern English:

> *A* Povre widwe, somdel stape in age,
> Was whylom dwelling in *a* narwe cotage,
> Besyde *a* grove, stonding in *a* dale[50]
>
> He was *a* wel good wrighte, *a* carpenter[51]
>
> he was *a* good felawe.[52]
>
> He yaf nat of that text *a* pulled hen,
> That seith, that hunters been nat holy men;
> Ne that *a* monk, whan he is cloisterlees,

---

[47] Mustanoja, *Middle English Syntax*, p. 260: "In Aelfric's writings, where *an* and *sum* are equally common, the instances of their individualising use amount to 398 and 326 and those of their generalising (generic) use to 33 and 54, according to ... P. Süsskand. At the end of the OE period *an* and *sum* are thus used primarily for purposes of individualisation."
[48] See Mustanoja, *op. cit.*, p. 261.
[49] P. Süsskand, *Geschichte des unbestimmten Artikels im Alt- und Frühmittelenglischen*, SEP LXXXV (Halle, 1935).
[50] Chaucer CT B NP 4011—4013.
[51] Chaucer CT A Prol 614.
[52] Chaucer CT A Prol 395.

Is lykned til *a* fish that is waterlees;
This is to seyn, *a* monk out of his cloistre.
But thilke text held he nat worth *an* oistre.[53]

E. FLUCTUATING USAGE

There has been, at all stages of the language, a certain amount of fluctuation in the usage of the article system, and an unsettled state of affairs in certain constructions, especially with proper nouns. In Chapter VI it will be shown that when an adjective is used with a proper noun, the use of an article determines the relationship of the adjective significate to the significate of the noun.[54] Sometimes the exact nature of this relationship may be unimportant; in such a case the usage may, in fact, be affected by problems of versification:

Wel knew he the olde Esculapius,
And Deyscorides, and eek Rufus,
Old Ypocras . . .[55]

In such a case as this, it makes but little difference whether the article is used or not.

Rank and titles have always caused a fluctuating usage. Chaucer spoke of

Th'olde dayes of the King Arthour[56]

whereas today we usually speak of *King Arthur*. But although we use no article with *King*, we normally do so with such titles as *Emperor, Archduke* and *Angel*:

the Emperor Claudius, the Archduke Ferdinand, the Angel Gabriel;

but one can also say (especially in American English):

Emperor Hirohito, Archduke Ferdinand of Austria.

Inversely *Lord* normally takes no article, but in very formal style we may say *the Lord Durham, the Lord Tweedsmuir*. The choice of one form or another would seem to depend on whether we accept the title as a separate common noun *(cf.* French: *le docteur Dupont)*, or as a part of the total name. We must be neither surprised nor shocked, therefore, at the variety of usage in Middle English for *prince, duke, knight, earl, pope, bishop, abbot. etc.*

Confusion of forms may even on occasion explain some inconsistent usages

[53] Chaucer CT A Prol 177—182.
[54] See pp. 106—107,.
[55] Chaucer CT A Prol 429—431.
[56] Chaucer CT D WB 857.

to be found throughout the history of the language. French *de* was sometimes translated *the*, giving rise to such peculiarities as

> *two lordes þe Mortymer (duo magnates de Mortuo Mari)*[57]

There is one interesting usage in Middle English that is not commonly found in Modern English: the use of the article with a non-numerical singular, especially in expressions of comparison:

> And like the burned gold was his colour[58]
> His bile was blak, and as the jeet it shoon[59]
> His comb was redder than the fyn coral[60]
> They were adrad of him as of the deeth[61]
> condemnyd to þe deþ[62]
> Ther was the revel and the melodye[63]
> the charite goth al unknowe[64]

Notice, however, the fluctuations in the following:

> Dark was the night as pitch or as the cole[65]
> tho was the vertu sett above And vice was put under fote[66]
> ...whyt as morne milk[67]

Such expressions normally use no article in Modern English:

> Red as blood
> Black as coal
> Hot as fire
> White as death

It has been assumed that this Middle English usage is due to the influence of French upon English. It must be observed, however, that it is the common usage of German and that it is not unknown in Modern English:

> White as the driven snow
> Black as the tar[68]
> It's like milk; just like the milk[69]

---

[57] "The Metrical Chronicle of Robert of Gloucester", 11134, qu. Mustanoja, *Middle English Syntax*, p. 234—5.
[58] Chaucer CT B NP 4054.
[59] Chaucer CT B NP 4051.
[60] Chaucer CT B NP 4049.
[61] Chaucer CT A Prol 605.
[62] Margery Kempe, 71, qu. Mustanoja, *op. cit.*, p. 257.
[63] Chaucer CT A Mil 3652.
[64] Gower, CA Prol 319 qu. Mustanoja, *op. cit.*, p. 257.
[65] Chaucer CT A Mil 3731.
[66] Gower, CA Prol 116, qu. Mustanoja, *op. cit.*, p. 257.
[67] Chaucer CT A Prol 358.
[68] Conversation: lady commenting on the state of her children.
[69] Conversation: gentleman commenting on the colour of carpet cement.

It would seem rather, that in this usage the actualising force of the article adds greater emphasis to the comparison,[70] and that this emphasis is at the discretion of the speaker, hence the fluctuations in both Middle English and Modern English. The fact that the article was more common in this usage in Middle English is relevant to the development of the zero article, which has gradually established itself, since the decay of the article morphology in early Middle English[71], as a vital means of representing the non-numerical singular: *chicken* (meat) as opposed to *the chicken* (the fowl). Only this fact can explain why the Modern English usage tends to be *away* from the use of the article in these expressions when the normal development of an article system is *towards* a more generalized usage. This development of the non-numerical force of the zero article also explains why *man* (in the sense of *mankind*) and sometimes *woman* take no article in Modern English, as opposed to other nouns of the same type:

> The cow is useful to the farmer.
> The telephone is useful to the businessman.
> The horse is useful to man.

whereas in Old English *mann* (in the sense of mankind) frequently (but not always) has an article:

> seo deah gehwæþer ge *þæs mannes* sawle ge his lichaman
> it is good both for *man's* soul and for his body[72]

In Middle English (with one or two exceptions), and in Modern English the noun *man* (and sometimes *woman*), when used in the generic sense, are given a non-numerical force by the use of article zero. This usage is bound up with the fact the speaker himself is *necessarily always* involved in the concept and cannot as readily detach himself and see it as a separate unit, such as *the horse, the telephone;* thus, we see *man* as a continuate, and woman frequently so (but not always)[73]. There are other interesting facts related to this phenomenon: the Latin noun *homo* evolves until it finally becomes in French an indefinite pronoun: *on* (it is the accusative *hominem* that gives us *homme*); the

---

[70]   *Cf.* the honorific use, as described in Chapter VI.
[71]   For the relevance of the decay of the morphology to this phenomenon, see below, pp. 180—181.
[72]   Example from *Sweet's Anglo Saxon Primer*, p. 49.
[73]   For a further and more detailed explanation, see pp. 125—126. By way of comparison, observe the following quotation from *The Screwtape Letters*, where the devil Screwtape is writing to his nephew, the devil Wormwood: "When *the humans* disbelieve in our existence we lose all the pleasing results." (Fontana Books ed., p. 39). The unusual use of the article here (unit reference) suggests the view of an outsider considering the unit from the exterior; a mere mortal (not being an outsider), would not have used an article. See also the comments, on page 91 concerning internal and external views.

etymological relationship of a similar pair (pronoun *man* and noun *mann)* in the Germanic languages (including Old English) is even more obvious. That this noun can so readily evolve into a pronoun demonstrates that it has unusual elements in its semantic content.[74]

Most fluctuations, whether at one period or at different periods, represent borderline cases that may be affected by stylistic, prosodic or other considerations; they should not blind us to the fact that there is, in fact, a continuously evolving article system and that, apart from those cases that fringe upon two distinct usages, the use of the article is consistent and systematic.

[74] Jespersen, *Philosophy of Grammar* (London, 1924), p. 204, comments that the main distinction between the noun and the pronoun is the force of stress, and that the Middle English form *men* used with a singular verb is undoubtedly a phonetically weakened form of the pronoun *man*.

THE METHOD

A. SCIENTIFIC METHOD: EMPIRICAL AND THEORETICAL

Science is a dynamism, a way of proceeding, not a subject matter; in science there is movement between the two poles of the empirical and the theoretical. Normally, the procedure begins with empirical observations, from which inferences can be made, and a hypothesis, or theory, proposed. In most cases, a hypothesis proposed in this way may only be considered scientific if it is treated to an imaginative and thorough appraisal by testing, experimentation and demonstration, during which evidence will be gathered to prove or disprove it. When it functions in this straightforward way, scientific methodology circulates continuously between the theoretical and the empirical; between the empirical *faits à expliquer* (facts to be explained) and the theoretical *fait explicateur* (fact which explains).[1] For a diagram, see Figure II.1.

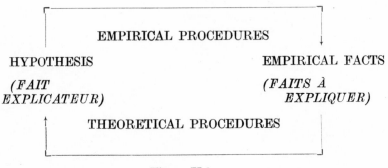

Figure II.1

Newton's discovery and elaboration of the theory of gravity is often cited as a classic example of the normal functioning of scientific method. Newton himself stated that "analysis consists in making ... observations, and in drawing general conclusions from them by induction ... And if no exceptions occur

---

[1] For an explanation of these terms and a discussion of the distinction, see R. Valin "Qu'est-ce qu'un fait linguistique?", in *Le Français moderne*, Vol. XXVII, pp. 85—93.

from phenomena, the conclusion may be pronounced generally."[2] His observations of falling objects led him to propose the theory of gravitation, but he abandoned his hypothesis when he found that the gravitational pull of the moon failed to agree with his prediction; his papers remained untouched in a drawer for twenty years until a French expedition made a more accurate survey of the circumference of the earth; at this point Newton realized that his original calculations had been based on erroneous information and that his theory was, in fact, justified. It is this classical view of science that is summed up in Einstein's famous dictum: "The grand aim of all science is to cover the greatest number of empirical facts by logical deduction from the smallest number of hypotheses or axioms."

Scientific method is therefore twofold: (1) it requires the making of explicative generalizations, and (2) it requires such generalizations to be demonstrated or proved. This may appear aphoristic, but it emphasizes that science is a procedure and not a subject matter, and such emphasis is necessary because of the claim that has sometimes been made that science has a restricted subject matter: the directly observable.[3] This claim is a misrepresentation: the directly observable is the necessary point of departure of scientific method, but scientific method, by its very nature, leads beyond the directly observable to the hypothesis or the hypothetical substructure, not directly observable, that lies behind the observable fact. To restrict the subject matter of science to the directly observable is to choose, deliberately, to avoid the scientific procedure of intuitive induction,[4] to refuse to make hypotheses.

B. EVIDENCE AND PROOF

Theoretical procedures produce hypotheses; empirical procedures produce evidence. True science requires both and depends for its rigour on the latter.[5] Evidence may be of two kinds, (1) direct, factual evidence (from observing a state of affairs, for example) and (2) indirect, circumstantial evidence (from

[2] Quoted in J. W. N. Sullivan, *The Limitations of Science*, Mentor Edition, 1949.
[3] "We have no right to guess about the linguistic workings of an inaccessible 'mind' and we can secure no advantage from such guesses. The linguistic processes of the 'mind' are quite simply unobservable . . . The scientific method is quite simply the convention that mind does not exist." W. Freeman Twaddell, *On Defining the Phoneme*, Language Monograph No. 16, (1935).
[4] See N. Chomsky, *Aspects of the Theory of Syntax* (M.I.T. Press, 1965), p. 193: "The behaviorist position is not an arguable matter. It is simply an expression of lack of interest in theory and explanation."
[5] "Ainsi que toute science, la science du langage a deux racines: une racine au *voir* et une racine au *concevoir* (au comprendre) qui sont pour elle sources de deux éclairements simultanés et inégaux — de la diathèse (de la combinaison arrangée) desquels elle tient sa puissance de pénétration du réel observé." Guillaume, *Langage et science du langage*, p.274.

observing the results or functioning of something that is not in itself directly observable, — for example a force). When evidence is of a logical nature (*i.e.*, a coherent network of necessary relationships) it may be said to constitute proof.

Guillaume, whose early training was in the mathematical and physical sciences, was fond of quoting the dictum of Meillet that science lives by proof, not truth. The distinction is important. Science does not concern itself with metaphysical value judgements as to the 'existence' of things, but rather with working models. If the models (*i.e.*, theories, hypotheses) are found to function with simplicity, elegance and rigour, then they are accepted as scientifically proved, not because they are 'true' in any sense, but because of the degree of their probability. They may eventually be replaced by models that are simpler, more elegant, or more rigorous. Given the nature of human knowledge, proof, in science, is a matter of probability, never of absolute certainty. *Provability* and *probability* have the same etymon.

The attitudes of the Neo-grammarians are revealing in this regard. They insisted that (i) a hypothesis should not be acceptable if there were any anomalies, but (ii) if acceptable, it should be accepted as a fact, not as a mere abstraction. In their view it was scandalous to accept a not fully consistent etymology and equally scandalous to believe that Proto-Indo-European was a mere imaginary 'scientific abstraction'. They held the middle view between the extremes of belief and unbelief.[6]

The principle hypothesis, the *fait explicateur*, of comparative grammar was, in fact, the existence of an Indo-European mother language;[7] the *faits à expliquer* were the correspondences between the languages of the Indo-European phylum; and the whole constituted a classic example of the functioning of scientific method.

C. GUILLAUME'S PSYCHOMECHANICS

The comparative method, often admired for its rigour and its elegance, served as a basis for Guillaume's earliest analyses. In *Le Problème de l'article* (1919) he spoke in the Foreword of "une grammaire comparative d'un autre ordre . . . au lieu de correspondances entre phonèmes, il s'agit de correspondances entre systèmes, — plus exactement entre les tendances communes à plusieurs systèmes . . ." Comparing these evolutive tendencies in different languages, he was able to glimpse their common intent, and observed:

---

[6]   Having placed their methodology on a more rigorous basis, they were more prepared to put their faith in its results.

[7]   Perhaps it should be pointed out that Proto-Indo-European is, to use Twaddell's term, "unobservable".

La leçon de correspondances entre matérialités de la langue est qu'un original commun a dû exister; celle qui se dégage de correspondances entre tendances syntaxiques est qu'un but commun est poursuivi. (p. 13)

Le Problème de l'article was dedicated to Meillet. Meillet, as we know, was a disciple of Saussure, and Saussure was a neo-grammarian. There is therefore much that is familiar in the work. But there are also signs of Guillaume's own originality: the word *discours* replaces the Saussurian term *parole;* there is mention of "la différence entre le nom dans la langue et le nom dans le discours" and this difference elsewhere brings forward the terms "puissance" (potentiality) and "effet" (actuality).

Ten years later in *Temps et Verbe* (1929) there is much more. There is a movement from *langue* to *discours*, from *puissance* to *effet* that is described as *génétique (i.e.,* generative) and that has its own underlying operative time: time for the operation of the creative, generative processes that result in discourse or speech.

In this way the static dualistic structuralism of Saussure is turned into a kinetic, monistic structuralism. Language *(le langage)* is seen as an activity that runs endlessly between the two poles of *langue* and *discours*, which become the opposite ends of a generative spectrum that he calls elsewhere the *acte de langage* (see Figure II.2).

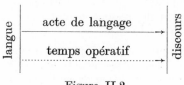

Figure II.2

Guillaume was, in fact, teaching a form of 'generative grammar' as early as the 1920's. But for all the surface resemblances,[8] there are fundamental differences between Guillaumian Psychomechanics and Transformational Grammar. The latter draws its basic inspiration from the procedures of mathematics, physics and cybernetics, and being a transcendence of American behaviourism[9] draws up its grammar on a descriptivist basis:

[8]   See Chomsky, *Aspects of the Theory of Syntax*, p. 4: "Hence in the technical sense, linguistic theory is mentalistic, since it is concerned with discovering a mental reality underlying actual behaviour . . . The distinction I am noting here is related to the *langue-parole* distinction of Saussure: but it is necessary to reject his concept of *langue* as merely a systematic inventory of items and return rather to the Humboldtian conception of underlying competence as a system of generative processes."
[9]   Most behaviurists, for example, treated the phoneme as an imaginary linguistic abstraction.

It seems to me that the most hopeful approach today is to describe the phenomena of language and of mental activity as accurately as possible, to try to develop an *abstract theoretical apparatus* that will as far as possible account for these phenomena and reveal the principles of their organization and functioning, without attempting, for the present, to relate the postulated mental structures and processes to any physiological mechanisms or to interpret mental function in terms of 'physical causes'.[10]

Guillaume, on the other hand, continuing the neo-grammarian tradition, insists that the task of the linguist is not "de théoriser le langage, mais de dire, l'ayant dans le langage même découverte, la théorie qu'il est."[11] Operative time is declared on Page 8 of *Temps et Verbe* to be *real* time, and a footnote adds the comment: "La pensée en action de langage exige réellement du temps." *Temps et Verbe* offers us, in fact, a working model of a real linguistic system,[12] a system of *la langue*, hypothetical to be sure, but simple, elegant, rigorous, and capable of explaining the multitudinous empirical facts of discourse. The system so offered is that of the French verb, along with a survey to show how the method applies to other Indo-European languages, and a demonstration of the common relevance of the same analytic elements.

Temps et Verbe closes with a methodological discussion, in which it is pointed out that such linguistic systems cannot be arrived at by direct observation:

Dès l'instant, en effet, que le langage est exprimé, ce qu'on a devant soi est de la pensée pensée. La pensée pensante, qui a créé cette pensée pensée, est close, morte. Et le linguiste qui se fie aux seules ressources de l'observation directe arrive inéluctablement trop tard pour s'en saisir.

Des moyens analytiques appropriés ont permis d'éviter cet écueil et l'on a pu ainsi étudier les formes dans leur phase génétique, antérieure à leur actualisation dans la parole, alors qu'il est de tradition de ne les considérer que dans leur phase de réalité, postérieure à cette actualisation. *(Temps et Verbe*, p. 134)

The description of such a system is in many ways the logical product of the methodological tradition of linguistics. The comparativists worked upstream in time from the directly observable daughter languages to the unobserved (and unobservable) proto-languages whose existence they considered necessary.

The same methodology has been applied in the twentieth century to the study of the phoneme. And if the majority of linguists did not realize that the phoneme was a mental entity, not directly observable, and attainable only by working upstream, so to speak, in operative time, the fact had not gone totally unobserved. Sapir, in his famous and germinal article on "The Psychological Reality of Phonemes" observed:

---

[10]   Chomsky, *Language and Mind* (1968), italics mine.

[11]   R. Valin, footnote on page 14 of the "Introduction" to Guillaume's posthumous *Langage et Science du Langage* (1964).

[12]   "... la réalité des opérations de pensée décrites ressort de leur nécessité, de ce qu'elles ne peuvent pas ne pas être ..." *(Temps et Verbe*, p. 133).

Some linguists seem to feel that the phoneme is a useful enough concept in an abstract theoretical discussion — in the theoretical presentation of the form of a language or in the comparison of related languages — but that it has small relevance for the actualities of speech. This point of view seems the reverse of realistic to the present writer. *(Selected Writings,* p. 46—7)

By a later comment in the same article he shows that his position parallels that of Guillaume: "Southern Paiute . . . is a language in which an unusually simple phonemic structure is actualized by a more than ordinarily complex phonetic one." The phonemic structure is the psychological reality, the "puissance"; the phonetic structure is the directly observable reality, the "effet". Furthermore the view that the phonemic structure "is actualized" suggests an activity, a movement from *puissance* to *effet* that parallels Guillaume's *acte de langage* with its underlying operative time.

The phoneme and the morpheme are, in this view, entities of tongue[13] *(i.e., langue), faits explicateurs.* Only allophones and allomorphs *actually* occur in discourse; they are the empirical *faits à expliquer.* In like manner only allosemes *(signifiés d'effet)* occur in discourse, actualizations of the (potential) sememes[14] *(signifiés de puissance)* that are stored in tongue. In other words, the so-called 'permanent' meaning of a word is the potential meaning available, of which any feature may be actualized to produce the alloseme or contextual meaning found in discourse. This simple and elegant view eliminates most disagreements over linguistic meaning by integrating them all within the compass of a single explanation.[15]

Guillaume finds it important, however, to distinguish two different levels in the potential significate, both of which are reflected in discourse: the material (or lexical) significate and the formal (or grammatical) significate. A material significate designates some conceptualized facet of the world of experience; a formal significate designates a conceptual position adopted within a grammatical system. In the combinations *table lamp* and *lamp table,* for example, the lexical elements are the same, but they are used in different grammatical

[13] Since the term *discours* is easily translatable whereas *parole* is not, it becomes fitting to use the English word 'discourse' instead of the French word. Likewise an extension of meaning may be given to English *tongue* similar to that which Saussure gave to French *langue.* This is all the more suitable in that the Saussurean and Guillaumian concepts are not compatible, since *tongue* stands for an operational dynamism, a system of systems, whereas Saussure's *langue* traditionally represents a static bundle of contrasts.

[14] The word *sememe* has here much the same sense as that implied by Bloomfield *(Language,* p. 162).

[15] The two types of significate occupy different positions *(i.e.,* moments) in the *acte de langage.* See R. Valin, *Petite introduction à la psychomécanique du langage* (Québec, 1955). The alloseme is of vital interest to translators: it is notable that a single word in one language can be translated in a multitude of different ways, depending on the precise nuance that fits into the context. The potential significate, in so far as it can be accurately described, is of importance to the lexicographer who must attempt to state the basic notion conveyed by the sign in order to give as complete an idea as possible of all the different contextual values that can be drawn from it.

functions. In short Guillaume would consider that in the sentence *Colourless green ideas sleep furiously* the grammatical forms are acceptable, but that they are filled with a lexical content that is largely nonsensical.

Chomsky has stated his opposition to this position, claiming that this reduces grammar "to such matters as government, agreement, inflectional paradigms, and the like. This decision seems to me no more defensible than a decision to restrict the study of language structure to phonetic patterning."[16] Two comments must be made. (1) Chomsky is justified in this view if he is countering Greenberg's statement (in H. Hoijer, *Language in Culture* (Chicago 1954), p. 156) that "... any language has a structural side and a semantic side, and it is possible to state them separately", and Hockett's "... the linguistic system of a language does not include the semantics" (Hoijer, *op. cit.*, p. 152); both statements which would reduce linguistics to a meaningless formalism. But (2) instead of differentiating formal meaning from lexical meaning, Chomsky englobes lexical meaning under "grammar", which is a swing to the opposite extreme.[17] Guillaume takes the middle way of including lexical meaning in the analysis, but differentiating it from formal or grammatical meaning. It follows that certain lexical contents are unsuitable to certain grammatical forms: in "remorse felt John", *remorse* is normally an unsuitable lexical content for this particular grammatical structure when *felt* is the verb, since such a connection between these two terms does not correlate to our experience of the universe. This type of resistance we shall call 'lexical clash'. In this view "the dog looks frightening" is grammatically and lexically satisfactory; "the dog looks barking" is grammatical but suffers from lexical clash; but "barking looks dog the" is not only lexically but grammatically unsatisfactory.

This integrated view of meaning as an elemental facet of language has not always met with full understanding, however. Linguists whose empirical bias sometimes leads them to overlook or ignore questions of meaning may even go so far as to conclude that psychomechanics is a theory of semantics:

It is a frankly mentalistic approach concerned with the study of units of meaning (called SIGNIFIÉS) and the semantic system (LANGUE) of which these units are the elements.[18]

This is a sweeping misrepresentation. Guillaume speaks of "l'idée, pièce maîtresse de notre enseignement, que la langue est un système de systèmes,"[19] and insists that "la langue est un système ... une représentation des moyens

---

[16]   Footnote on pages 7 and 8 of *Current Issues in Linguistic Theory* (The Hague, 1966).
[17]   Since, however, transformational grammar seems to classify lexicon, morphology and syntax all as 'syntax', this may be a mere question of labels, which is not an arguable matter.
[18]   Margaret Langdon, in *International Journal of American Linguistics*, XXXII, p. 410.
[19]   Guillaume, *Langage et Science du Langage*, p. 223.

formels mécaniquement liés, faisant un tout mécanique cohérent . . ."[20] The notion of "langue" as a mere semantic system is completely inadequate and indefensible and would have been categorically rejected by Guillaume.

In the generative processes there is normally an automatic reflex between sememe and morpheme; the morpheme then becomes actualised as an allomorph which, on being released into the stream of speech presents the alloseme appropriate to the context and situation:

$$\text{SEMEME} \rightarrow \text{MORPHEME} \rangle \text{ALLOMORPH} \rightarrow \text{ALLOSEME}$$

Guillaume's terminology is as follows:

$$\text{SIGNIFIÉ DE PUISSANCE} \rightarrow \text{SIGNE DE PUISSANCE} \rangle \text{SIGNE D'EFFET} \rightarrow \text{SIGNIFIÉ D'EFFET}$$

(The *signe de puissance* is the equivalent of Saussure's *image acoustique* or *signifiant*.)[21]

It is of interest to examine the ideas and experiments of Penfield in connection with the above figure:

(Case C.H.) When the electrode was applied to point 26 on an anterior speech area, the patient was being shown a picture of a human foot. He said, 'Oh, I know what it is. That is what you put in your shoes.' After the electrode was withdrawn he said 'foot'.

When the electrode was applied to the supramarginal gyrus at 27, he said, 'I know what it is' and was silent. When the electrode was withdrawn, he said at once, 'tree', which was correct.[22]

What C. H. said suggests that an individual normally presents a concept to the speech mechanism and expects an answer. The concept may be an animal, a city, a type of action, or a quality. Each concept calls for a name. These names are wanted for what may be a noun or a verb, an adjective or an adverb.[23]

Whenever a man speaks or writes, he must first select the concepts that best serve his purpose from a conceptual mechanism. *Conceptual mechanism* seems a better expression than conceptual store-house, but neither term should suggest that the place of storing or the manner of activating is understood. Nevertheless, the study of aphasics shows clearly that the speech mechanism is separable from it. This necessitates the hypothesis that there is a conceptual store-house.[24]

[20] Guillaume, *Langage et Science du Langage*, p. 221.
[21] Guillaume changes the unsatisfactory Saussurean terminology. An *image acoustique* or mere phonemic shape is, strictly speaking, an *insignifiant*. See also the discussion below on the term *signifiant*.
[22] W. Penfield and L. Roberts, *Speech and Brain Mechanisms* (Princeton University Press, 1959), p. 227.
[23] Penfield and Roberts, *op. cit.*, p. 228.
[24] Penfield and Roberts, *op. cit.*, p. 233.

In comparing Penfield's explanation with Guillaume's we see that the potential significate or sememe is a concept in the 'concept mechanism'. Unless blocked by an electrical discharge, this concept mechanism will automatically activate the 'speech mechanism' and release the 'name' *(i.e.,* sign or morpheme).[25]

From here it follows that the releasing of the sign into the stream of speech gives it its meaning in the sentence, a meaning which has so often, and rightly, been described as contextual. It is the sign which in this way delivers the actual significate, which will be restricted by context, but will only be, can only be, what the potential significate allows it to be; a meaning not inherent in the potential significate would be an impossibility.

It remains for us to clarify the nature of the *signifiant* or significant. The sense of the term itself is somewhat abused by the Saussurean meaning of acoustic-image-without-meaning, for a sign is only significant when one knows its meaning. In Guillaumian terminology, therefore, the significant is the sign plus its significate. There are, necessarily, two types of significant: (a) the *signifiant de puissance* (potential significant), which is the result of that permanent connection (for the individual) of the sign and its potential significate noted by Penfield, and (b) the *signifiant d'effet* (actual significant) which is the momentary bond between the sign and its contextual sense in the stream of speech (see Figure II.3).

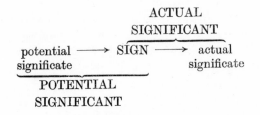

Figure II.3

These terms are necessary to describe two different states of the full word (name + sense in Ullmann's terminology): the potential full word (potential significant) and the actual full word when used in the stream of speech (actual significant).

We must not complain of these dichotomies.[26] The distinction between the two levels of tongue and discourse is essential to all linguistic analysis; it is a

---

[25] "The connection between *speech mechanism* and *concept mechanism* is evidently reflex and automatic." Penfield and Roberts, *op. cit.,* p. 234.
[26] *Cf.* J. R. Firth, *Papers in Linguistics,* p. 227.

distinction between two orders of fact. If we ignore this distinction we are confronted with two alternatives. One is to make ambiguous and confusing statements, as when we make use of the noun *word* without clarifying whether we mean *potential significant* or *actual significant*. This gives rise to much confusion, argument, and quarreling:

A word on its own is not meaningful; what it means depends on its context.[27]
There is no getting away from the fact that single words have more or less permanent meanings.[28]

This is, of course, the old quarrel over *contextual* and *permanent* meaning.

The second alternative is to describe and analyse only the directly observable aspects of language that appertain to the level of discourse and to ignore the mental aspects to be found at the level of tongue, aspects that, like the workings of the atom, can only be approached through indirect evidence: the entities of tongue, and the entities of discourse belong, like magnetism and the magnetic field, to different orders of fact.[29] The second solution is satisfactory only if we make no claim to be analysing and describing *language;* if we do make such a claim, we must be careful to investigate all facets of language, the hidden as well as the obvious.[30]

D. THE NATURE OF LANGUAGE: THE GUILLAUMIAN VIEW

We must beware of accepting that which is merely obvious at its face value, and search always for a more and more penetrating analysis of fact, the substructure that is lurking behind the obvious. It is obvious, for example, that language is a system of communication. It is not sufficient as a verbal definition, however, to *define* language as a system of communication. There are many other systems of communication, non-linguistic as well as linguistic; we must be able to say in what way human language differs from these other systems. Nor is it sufficient to say that language is simply sound that has meaning (although the fact is equally obvious); the barking of a dog or the wailing of a siren are also sounds that have meaning, but neither is linguistic. Nor is language a code, since a code necessarily has a one-to-one relationship with the codified text; no such relationship is to be found in language — even when

---

[27]   W. H. Mittins, *A Grammar of Modern English* (London, 1962), p. 1.
[28]   G. Stern, *Meaning and Changes of Meaning* (Goteburg, 1931), p. 85.
[29]   The morpheme and the phoneme are entities of *tongue, faits explicateurs*, theoretical. Only allomorphs and allophones *actually* occur in discourse; there are many obvious implications of this.
[30]   S. Ullmann, *Principles of Semantics* (Oxford, 1957), p. 321, makes the same point: "In fact such a conception of linguistics would not even be truly scientific, for it is a *sine qua non* of scientific method that it should be commensurate to the subject matter."

translating from one language to another — because of the prolific variation caused by situational context, the bane of all translators and the stumbling block to machine translation.[31] Observation and reflexion reveal that language is, first and foremost, a conventional analysis and categorization of our impressions of the world of reality — a fact that is not immediately obvious and that requires some elucidation.

All human language is a means of expressing coherently man's multifold and ephemeral impressions of the universe in which he lives. For any coherent expression of such impressions to take place, certain conditions must be fulfilled. The chaos of our experiences must be reduced to order, must be structured; in order to do this we must have at our disposal a mechanism, a ready-made means of constructing; furthermore, this means of constructing must exist prior to any attempt at structuring which in turn must take place before any attempt at expression.[32] Guillaume sums up these conditions in a succinct formula:

$$indicible \;\rightarrow\; dicible \;\rightarrow\; dire \;\rightarrow\; dit$$

What is *unsayable* must first be made *sayable*; an act of *saying* may then ensue and will result in something *said*.

The *unsayable* or *indicible* is the multiplicity and variety of our experiences of the universe, experiences that are, strictly speaking, never repeated. Everything, to quote Heraclitus, is in a state of flux.[33] The same philosopher in another fragment cryptically remarks, "You cannot put your foot into the same river twice", which has been wittily amended to read, "You cannot put your foot into the same river once." Although Heraclitus proposed it six hundred years B.C., it has taken hundreds of years of philosophizing to realize the importance of the fact that the world is in a state of perpetual change.[34] The philosophy of becoming, as opposed to that of being, is relatively new, but the most recent twentieth century thought is much concerned with movement, genesis, evolution, time.[35] Just as experience is non-recurring, similar objects

---

[31] *Je parle* means: I talk, I speak, I am talking, I am speaking, I do talk, I do speak, I have talked, I have spoken, I have been talking, I have been speaking (depending on context).

[32] We are well aware that these conditions do not prevail for incoherent expressions of reality, the means of which is shared by man and the animal kingdom: howls of rage, screams of pain, cries of fear, murmurs of pleasure, etc.

[33] Heraclitus did not mean by this that everything is in a state of confusion; his doctrine of the *logos* marks the beginning in European thought of the notion of an organized and rational order behind the universe.

[34] The paradox of Achilles and the tortoise shows that the Greeks certainly had not learned to apply the principle.

[35] In dealing so comprehensibly with these themes, Guillaume was much ahead of his time; this partially explains the incomprehension of many of his contemporaries, who could not understand what he was attempting.

are never identical; even those that look alike occupy different positions in the space/time continuum. But we do not, cannot in fact, call all similar objects by different names, nor change these names for every second (or even year!) of their existence. Spatio-temporal experience and its contents are therefore 'unsayable' (indicible) and the function of tongue is to provide a means of organizing such experience, thereby making it expressible. This results in the grouping and categorization of immediate experiences[36] to provide a lexicon, and the structuring of spatio-temporal experience to form a grammar. It is in this way that tongue comes into existence, as a *système de dicibilités*, a potentiality of expression, without which the universe and our experience of it could not be discussed coherently, nor even conceived. Without tongue, discourse would be incoherent, chaotic.

The function of tongue, therefore, is to provide a means of representing experience. Consequently, in Guillaume's view the language act *(acte de langage)* has two distinguishable moments: an act of representation made possible by the systems of tongue, and an act of expression made possible by the preceding act of representation. In such a view, tongue as an entity is a potentiality of movement; discourse as an entity is a result of movement[37] (see Figure II.4).[38]

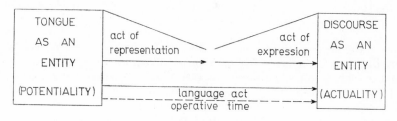

Figure II.4

Guillaume proposes that, in languages of the Indo-European type, the act of representation is the genesis of the word-schema and the act of expression is the genesis of the sentence-schema.[39] This rather surprising proposal is supported by the following evidence:

[36] This categorization of our impressions is the fact of language that lies behind Trier's 'field theory' of semantics. In order to make the universe 'thinkable', each language divides it into different segments or concepts. Since there are many ways of dividing the whole coherently, the concepts of one language will not necessarily correspond with those of another, nor even with those of the same language at a different historical date.

[37] The conclusion to be drawn from such a view is that the structures of tongue are operational, and must therefore be described in dynamic, not static terms.

[38] *Cf.* R. Valin, *Petite introduction*, p. 48.

[39] *Cf.* R. Valin, *Petite introduction*, pp. 60—80.

(i) The word and the sentence are the two essential realities of all human language. Both are actualised by means of generative processes, but the processes are obviously different since a sentence is generated from words: we talk of "finding the right words".

(ii) In the Indo-European languages, where the word is clearly distinguishable from the sentence, there is a much greater freedom in the structure of the sentence than in the structure of the word. The rigidity found in the grammar of the word reflects the fact that this grammar is located in the institutional side of language (tongue).[40] The freedom enjoyed by the speaker in constructing the sentence as he pleases is inhibited only by the syntactic patterns, which in turn are dependent upon the grammar of the word; this freedom reflects the ephemeral character of discourse — there is nothing in tongue that determines the length of a sentence!

(iii) The word exists in both tongue and discourse but the sentence exists only in discourse. The dictionary of an Indo-European language will contain a certain number of words, but there is no limit to the number of possible sentences, and a 'dictionary' of sentences is unthinkable.

(iv) Remarkably enough, precisely the same point of view has been expressed by the famous British neuro-surgeon Russell Brain (later Lord Brain). In an article in *Archivum Linguisticum* entitled "The Semantic Aspect of Aphasia",[41] he states his case as follows:

> In speech the nervous system has to deal with sentence-schemas as well as word-schemas. But the word-schema is a more or less fixed, atomic element in the brain, the sentence-schema in spoken speech is, as it were, molecular, being built up in the actual process of speech out of word-schemas, and demolished as soon as it has served its purpose, which is to evoke its meaning. Thus the word is the unit of language and the sentence is the unit of speech.

E. THE INTUITIONAL MECHANISM, FUNDAMENTAL PRINCIPLE OF THE LINGUISTIC BINARY UNIT

It is a thesis of Guillaume that the binary contrasts to be found in the grammatical structure of a language are a reflection of a fundamental intuitional mechanism: the relationship of the greater and the less, the particular and the general, the dialogue of man and the universe. The representation of the relationship between two determinants such as these must be binary: the relationship between father and son may be seen under either its filial or its paternal aspect; the relationship of any other two determinants is dual, or

---

[40]   If the word is a 'minimum free form' it is because anything less than the minimum is 'bound'.

[41]   *Archivum Linguisticum*, Vol. 8, 1: 20—27.

binary, in the same way. Furthermore, the inverse movement or aspect is not simply a return to base along the same channel, but a separate movement or aspect of its own and should be represented as such. The dynamic relationship of two terms A and B is best represented as follows:

$$\underline{A_1 \rightarrow B_1 \quad B_2 \rightarrow A_2}$$

A_1 is determinant A seen as a *terminus a quo;* as A_2 it is seen as a *terminus ad quem.*[42] B_1 and B_2 are respectively *terminus ad quem* and *terminus a quo.*

It is axiomatic that we think by contrast, being unable to do otherwise. English as a natural language reflects this fact not only in the lexicon, but also in the binary oppositions to be found among the grammatical structures. Because of this we shall find the presented figure (Figure II.5) of the structural binary unit or *tenseur binaire radicale* repeated time and again in psychomechanical analysis.

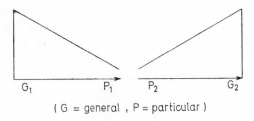

(G = general , P = particular)

Figure II.5

This fundamental binary contrast is, in Guillaume's view, the basic intuitional mechanism of the Indo-European languages, having its origin in the interplay of the relationship between man and the universe in which he finds himself (Figure II.6).

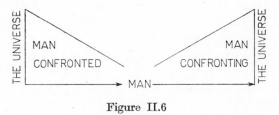

Figure II.6

This view, rather startling at first sight, would seem to be borne out by a variety of supporting evidence:

[42] *Terminus a quo* is the terminal point of departure: *terminus ad quem* terminal point of arrival.

(i) The number of binary oppositions to be found that reflect this relationship. Some examples: singular — plural,[43] passive — active,[44] predicate — subject.[45] Other, more detailed, examples will be presented later.[46]

(ii) That these two views are a fundamental part of our mental outlook is supported by the fact that psychologists have found it necessary to make a binary division in the function or processes of consciousness and that this division (cognition/conation) reflects the schema above: the first part (man confronted) corresponds to *cognition*, the second (man confronting) to *conation*.

(iii) The human mind, confronted with the totality of the universe, makes a basic binary division or dichotomy of what scientists think to be a continuum, thus forming the contrasting notions of space and time from the space-time continuum.[47]

(iv) The binary nature of the processes of the neural system has been commented upon by Wiener:[48] "From that time, it became clear to us that the ultra-rapid computing machine, depending as it does on consecutive switching devices, must represent almost an ideal model of the problems arising in the nervous system. The all-or-nothing character of the discharge of the neurons is precisely analogous to the single choice made in determining a digit on the binary scale, which more than one of us had already contemplated as the most satisfactory basis of computing machine design."

F. DEMATERIALIZATION AND EVOLUTION

In discussing the systemic nature of tongue,[49] Guillaume proposes that it be considered as a concentric successivity of systems, each enclosed in the other, and that there is an inherent tendency to reduce the material content of these systems following an anti-substantial movement away from the periphery. In linguistic evolution, this results in the construction of (more abstract) systems toward the centre which make possible a more and more generalized grasp of reality. We can see this working out in the gradual de-substantiation or dematerialization of the noun in French during its centuries of evolution at the same time as the creation of an article system, the apo-

---

[43] The individual man is a singular amid the plurality of the universe.
[44] *Confronted* is passive; *confronting* is active.
[45] A predicate is contingent upon its supporting subject (predicate = borne; subject = bearer).
[46] See, for example, the explanation of English demonstratives at the end of Chapter IV.
[47] See also Guillaume, *L'Architectonique du temps dans les langues classiques* (Copenhagen, 1945), pp. 9—10, esp., "Toute l'activité de l'esprit humain, consciente ou inconsciente, repose sur la puissance qu'il possède de se porter, en toute occasion, du côté du plus ou du côté du moins particulier."
[48] Norbert Wiener, *Cybernetics* (MIT Press, 2nd ed. 1961), p. 14.
[49] See Guillaume, *La Langue est-elle ou n'est-elle pas un système?* (Québec, 1952).

theosis of de-substantiated systems. Loss of case in the noun is also an anti-substantial movement, and it, in turn, is accompanied by the development of the system of prepositions. In similar fashion the loss of personal endings and aspect markers in the verb is accompanied by the rise of a system of dematerialized auxiliaries; what shred of the notion of possession remains in the *have* of *I have spoken*?

G. MENTALISM AND MECHANISM

Guillaume, obviously, was an avowed mentalist, but his mentalism is not a kind that would come under Bloomfield's famous censure,[50] since it is also mechanistic. The justification of this new style of mechanism has been made by Katz,[51] and Wiener observes that the mechanist-mentalist controversy is now largely a dead issue.[52]

Vitalism has won to the extent that even mechanisms correspond to the time-structure of vitalisms; but as we have said, this victory is a complete defeat, for from every point of view which has the slightest relation to morality or religion, the new mechanics is fully as mechanistic as the old . . . In fact, the whole mechanist-vitalist controversy has been relegated to the limbo of badly posed questions.

Most intellectual controversies of any account, whether they be twelfth century arguments of realist versus nominalist or twentieth century arguments of behaviorist versus phenomenologist, can be seen as the choosing of opposing approaches or aspects of a monism that has been binarily analysed; in such cases the argument may be eliminated by integration within a monistic view: such, for example, is the case of permanent and contextual meaning, as described above.

The monistic approach is therefore important; but so also is the dynamic approach, which eliminates arguments concerning whether a subject matter is 'knowable' or 'unknowable'. There are many dynamic substructures in science for which we have no direct evidence;[53] all that scientific method requires as evidence for the *existence* of such entities is that they should form part of a rigorously coherent and productive theory.

---

[50] L. Bloomfield, *Language* (New York, 1933), p. 32.
[51] J. J. Katz, "Mentalism in Linguistics", in *Language* 40, No. 2 (1964), pp. 124—137.
[52] N. Wiener, *Cybernetics*, p. 44. For another expression of this point of view see Chomsky, *Aspects of the Theory of Syntax*, pp. 193—194.
[53] "Upon examination such concepts as gravitation, electromagnetism, energy, current, momentum, the atom, the neutron, all turn out to be theoretical substructures, inventions, metaphors which man's intellect has contrived to help him picture the true, the objective reality he apprehends beneath the surface of things." L. Barnet, *The Universe and Dr. Einstein*, p. 115.

H. OPERATIVE TIME

Zeno the Eleatic, the founder of the dialectic method, was also the originator of a variety of paradoxes, some ingenious, some not so ingenious. One of the most ingenious was that of the flying arrow: since the arrow at each moment is simply where it is, the arrow in flight is always at rest. Bergson calls this view cinematographic; it is, he says, natural to the intellect, but radically vicious. But he meets the argument by denying that the arrow is ever anywhere, which is also a paradox.

The confusion here is essentially one of time and space. Zeno takes the spatial view that there is a *thing* and abstracts the element of time; Bergson takes the temporal view that there is *motion* and abstracts the element of space.[54] A post-Einsteinian view eliminates the argument by englobing both views within the wider range of the space-time continuum: there *is* a thing, but since *being* itself is dynamic, not static, it is perfectly plausible for the thing to be dynamically 'in motion' or dynamically 'at rest', or even, dynamically 'coming to rest'.

Since Saussure, the temporal view of language has been called diachronic, and the spatial (*i.e.*, static) view synchronic. Guillaume's notion of operative time is essentially the insight that the synchronic view is no more static than the motion arrested by the camera shutter: that the synchronic must be discussed in temporal as well as spatial terms, that the Einsteinian view of a space/time continuum must be applied to the study of language, that language (*langage*) is an activity, a dynamism, a monism, and that the static dualism of Saussure is not a true reflection of reality any more than is Zeno's arrow. In other words the phoneme (entity of tongue) and the allophone (entity of discourse) are not two different things, but two different temporal aspects of one and the same thing.

It appears that, for some, this is a difficult idea to grasp. In a recent review the notion of operative time is criticized as follows:[55]

I do not propose to discuss Guillaume's views in detail, but only to point out two facts which seem to me basic in relation to them. First, I fail to see how the introduction of the notion of time in the synchronic consideration of linguistic phenomena represents anything but a reversion to pre-Saussurean times. No one denies that the SPEECH ACT takes time to occur, but on the other hand the methodological irrele-

---

[54]   The arrow in Zeno's view is 'seen' in space but not in time; in Bergson's view is 'seen' in time but not in space. Zeno's mistake was to presume that a 'view' (or point of time) is static; any photographer can demonstrate the fallacy of such a presumption. Extra high speed of a camera shutter does not arrest movement, but brings it within manageable proportions, since, no matter how small the space of time, movement is possible within it — if the space of time is reduced to zero, no view results. Neither the static positions of Zeno nor the bodyless motion of Bergson correspond to reality.

[55]   Heles Contreras, in *Language* 42: 106—8.

vance of time for the understanding of a linguistic SYSTEM is accepted as axiomatic by most linguists. Second, and most important, Guillaume's views fall into the category of Joos's 'invulnerable theories'; since they depend entirely on the analyst's intuition. They are thus all but useless, since they cannot be proved true or false.

Such incomprehension, understandable only in so far as the significance of the notions of post-Einsteinian physics will take time to penetrate the whole of the intellectual spectrum,[56] ignores the fact that Guillaume's notion of operative time is a transcendence of the Saussurean view and draws its inspiration from twentieth century physics.[57] Furthermore, the argument that most linguists consider it irrelevant is merely to state the *status quo;* if this were to be considered a justification, all new ideas must automatically (and axiomatically) be rejected: the criticism itself is irrelevant.

The second point is a grave misrepresentation, probably due to the common misunderstanding, noted above, of the scientific operation known as *intuitive induction*, which is the keystone to Guillaume's procedure. The validity of an intuitive hypothesis does not depend "entirely on the analyst's intuition"; its validity depends upon evidence. It took Newton, as we have seen, twenty years before final elaboration and demonstration of the theory of gravitation. It has taken a century to demonstrate the validity of the theory of evolution (itself based on a very remarkable intuition), and a generation to verify the hypotheses of Einstein; in both these latter instances there was considerable opposition, based on either incomprehension or *parti pris*.

Many of the implications of Guillaume's theories have not yet been worked out, but his work nevertheless represents a major step forward in the penetration of some of the most difficult and hitherto hidden areas of language. Its relevance must be evaluated in the light of what it aims to do and within the background of a broad philosophy of language. To criticize it in the light of any other scheme of values is to do it considerably less than justice.

I. MODELS

The study of language has always been accompanied by the problem of the metalanguage: the language used to describe or discuss the language under study. There is a danger in linguistic analysis that the metalanguage may become elaborated to the detriment of the analysis itself. Traditional language learning, for example, has often come under this stricture: class time is largely

---

[56] The rejection of operative time is itself, ironically, a return to pre-Einsteinian times.
[57] Anyone brought up on Euclid would have the same kind of difficulty accepting that the sum of the angles of a triangle can be greater or less than 180°, and yet non-Euclidean geometry is, we are told, more relevant to reality than that of Euclid.

wasted when spent in discussion of the metalanguage rather than in involvement with the language being studied.

The three canons of science, according to Robins,[58] are Exhaustiveness, Consistency, and Economy of Statement. Since scientific method is so essentially involved with the building of hypothetical, explicative models, the type of model constructed will have a marked effect on the third canon, Economy of Statement, the canon that is concerned with the elaboration of the metalanguage.

It would seem from his own statements[59] that Guillaume was attempting to construct a grammar of "explanatory adequacy"[60] in at least one area of language. A measure of his success with the verb systems of French, Latin and Greek may be deduced from the fact that his models are exhaustive,[61] consistent[62] and so simple that they may be sketched on a single page. It may also be said that the elements of these models: *immanence/transcendence, incidence/decadence*, etc., have linguistic universality insofar as they are the elements from which other systems and grammars are constructed. These are, in short, the universal mechanisms from which grammars (in the Guillaumian sense) are constructed. In these terms there is no Universal Grammar, there are only different grammars that are differing arrangements of various universal mechanisms.[63]

J. DISCOVERY PROCEDURES

Statements of discovery procedures also constitute a further elaboration of the metalanguage without necessarily revealing anything significant about the language under study. Chomsky, in *Syntactic Structures*, expressly renounces, in fact, any statement of discovery procedures (pp. 52—3):

I think that it is very questionable that this goal is attainable in any interesting way, and I suspect that any attempt to meet it will lead into a maze of more and more complex analytic procedures that will fail to provide answers for many important questions about the nature of linguistic structure.

[58]   R. H. Robins, *General Linguistics: An Introductory Survey* (Longmans 1964), p. 8.
[59]   See, for example, the quotation above from p. 134 of *Temps et Verbe*.
[60]   See Chomsky, *Current Issues*, pp. 28—30.
[61]   He set himself to explain *all* usage.
[62]   All usages of a grammatical morpheme, however inconsistent on the surface, are explained as deriving from a single basic structure in tongue.
[63]   To use an analogy as clarification: there is no universal means of transportation; there are only different means of transportation (airplane, car, bicycle) that are constructed by utilizing certain universal mechanical principles, *e.g.*, the wheel, the lever.

And again on page 56, he adds:

> we shall never consider the question of how one might have arrived at the grammar whose simplicity is being determined ... Questions of this sort are not relevant to the program of research we have outlined above.

To this we may add that concern over discovery procedures is often associated with a wish to reduce the intellect to a purely mechanical technique. There is a concomitant danger of eliminating the watchdog of intelligence, so that the final result is a mere elaboration of the obvious.

It would seem, furthermore, that exaggerated scruple about minor methodological matters often accompanies the replacing of traditional linguistic terms by an esoteric jargon; both would seem to spring from an excessively defensive reaction on the part of those who find it important to claim that linguistics is a science, but who have not realized that science is a fundamental way of proceeding, not a subject matter. The comparative grammarians of the nineteenth century long ago established linguistics as a science,[64] and it would seem not at all inappropriate to continue, where possible, a traditional terminology in much grammatical description. Neologisms are then justified only when new concepts are developed and brought to light. If this proposal is followed, there should ensue not only the growing development of a traditional mainstream of scholarship (which might otherwise be in danger of being forgotten or ignored), but also less likelihood of following a current fashion or school (which might well lead only to a backwater).

[64] For a demonstration of this point see R. Valin, *La méthode comparative en linguistique historique et en psychomécanique du langage* (Quebec, 1964).

III

THE THEORY OF THE NOUN

A. THE NATURE OF THE NOUN

A noun is a sign used to refer to entities as if they were substances, *i.e.*, as if they had dimension within the space-time continuum.[1] We can see this quite clearly in the modifications of sense caused by juxtaposed adjectives. Few adjectives can be applied to all nouns because of lexical clash *(pink generosity*, for example) but the adjectives that seem universally applicable are adjectives of dimension such as *long* and *short*. The entity represented in *long road* is felt to have dimension in space; that represented in *long generosity* is felt to have dimension in time.

Being the linguistic means whereby elements of the universe[2] are represented as substantial, the signs of an Indo-European language that fit into the nominal pattern are usually sufficiently copious to overshadow those that fit into other categories (verb, adjective, etc.). It is within the framework of nominal expression also that there is the greatest frequency of borrowing, semantic shift and the creation of neologisms.

We are used to distinguishing between various types of noun: proper, common, abstract and concrete. Paul Christophersen, in his book *The Articles*,[3] uses further categories: collectives, uniques, toto-generic, pseudo-generic, and parti-generic nouns. These categories are misleading for three reasons. (i) No noun fits absolutely into any one category. Christophersen asserts that *weather* is "never thought of as unlimited in space or time",[4] and has, therefore, no toto-generic form. But one can discuss "weather as a facet of climate" in precisely this sense, using a 'toto-generic' *(i.e.*, zero article) form. He also lists *water* and *butter* as having no plural; *waters* is reasonably common in English: "Waters on a starry night / Are beautiful and fair".[5] *Butters* may be used in

---

[1] "The noun is commonly misdefined as the name of a person, place or thing. This is erroneous because grammar does not define with reference to external reality; it must define rather how reality is represented or signified. The noun is a word which designates something as a thing." J. Gallup, "An approach to the theory of declension", *Canadian Journal of Linguistics*, Vol. 8, No. 1 (1962), pp. 26—32.

[2] *i.e.*, experiential elements of reality.

[3] Paul Christophersen, *The Articles* (London and Copenhagen, 1939).

[4] Christophersen, *op. cit.*, p. 35.

[5] Wordsworth, *Intimations of Immortality*.

such a sentence as "One now has a choice of two butters, the salted and the salt-free". (ii) Almost all nouns can, in fact be used in almost all of these senses.[6] Not all these senses will correspond to facets of objective reality, but more will seem perfectly reasonable than the immediately obvious ones. Christophersen gives a list of nouns that "have normally no zero-form: book, page, letter, word, pen, cupboard, floor, girl, flower, street, tram, event, hour, plan, etc.",[7] but the following examples will suffice to show the inexactitude of the classification:

(1) They managed to clear a wide expanse of *floor*.
(2) A short length of *street* was taken up.
(3) *Letter* was the one means of communication he had.
(4) *Event* is the empirical basis of historical studies.

(iii) These categories are frequently non-linguistic; *i.e.*, they are not categories at the level of tongue. To make statements about the exterior world that is reflected in language is not necessarily to make statements about language. When Christophersen calls *the man in the moon* a unique, we must realize that it is only unique because of the external situation; there is nothing linguistically unique in either the representation or the expression. If we are to take situation regularly into account, then we can easily imagine a situation where *the man next door* becomes a unique.[8] Likewise, to say, as Christophersen does, that *letter* commonly has no zero-form is merely to say that when we use the concept (in the singular) we are commonly thinking of a singular physical object: *A letter arrived this morning*. This gives us no information about the noun itself, but merely a limited statement about its use, and does not, cannot, explain *Letter as a means of communication*, where the noun refers not to a concrete entity, but to an abstraction. The actual significate may be changed, but is, in each case, drawn from the same potential significate.

This potential significate cannot, by nature, be any less virtual or dematerialized in sense than the most abstract actual significate possible in discourse, since an actual significate can only be what the potential significate allows it to be. We have therefore a progression of the possible values that may be drawn from the potential significate, all the way from the very general: *Letter was*

---

[6] A distinctive subgroup, however, because of some distinctive semantic feature, resists all expression of number, singular or plural: toast, advice, machinery, luggage, luck (*cf.* misfortune), fun, etc. Number is expressed by means of a *measure:* a bit of luck, several pieces of toast. Chinese, which has no morphology of number in the noun at all uses measures in similar fashion: *one lump money* means one dollar; *two piece man* means two men.

[7] Christophersen, *op. cit.*, p. 24.

[8] *Cf.* Jespersen, *Philosophy of Grammar*, p. 109: "There is no reason for singling out a class of persons or things which are unique in themselves."

the one means of communication he had, to the very particular: *A letter arrived
this morning.* These values reflect the basic contrasting movements of particularization and generalization which are to be found throughout human thought
and language,[9] and which may be represented as a binary contrast at the level
of tongue (Figure III.1).

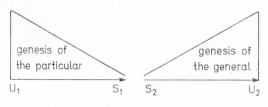

Figure III.1

Philosophers have been aware for centuries that common terms have two distinct types of meaning: denotation and connotation. Denotation points the
finger at the individual; connotation seeks the universal, generic sense of the
word. These two terms are a reflection of the binary discussion of values to be
found in the potential significate of the noun. However philosophers disagree
as to the exact meanings of the terms; many refuse to use them altogether
because of their ambiguity. Furthermore, if we try to fit them into the present
analysis, we shall find that it is possible to locate both denotation and connotation in both parts of the binary unit. It is also worth pointing out that the
philosopher is frequently more interested in the universe, the exterior experiential world, than in the linguistic means of representing the universe; for
the philosopher the *man in the moon* may well be, in logical terms, a unique.
Linguistics and logic are notoriously bad bed-follows, and the only reason for
introducing the notions of denotation and connotation at this point is to
emphasize that the binary nature of the potential significate of the noun in the
Indo-European languages has been observed and known for almost two and
a half millenia.

The values discussed in this binary unit are the *import* or horizon of meaning,
and the *support* or base.[10] The genesis of the particular is a movement toward
the support or basic sense of the noun (Figure III.2).

---

[9] See above pp. 30—32.
[10] *Import* and *support* are translations of the terms *apport* and *support* that Guillaume
uses in discussing the relationship of adjective and noun (see below). An attempt is made
here to delineate the functioning of the mechanism that gives the noun its "internal
incidence" and thereby, it is hoped, to shed light on Guillaume's concept of "extensivity".

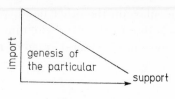

Figure III.2

The genesis of the general, on the other hand, is a movement toward the *import* or distant horizon of sense (Figure III.3).

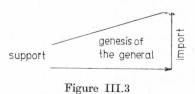

Figure III.3

We have seen that there is, in the linguistic evolution of the Indo-European languages, a natural tendency toward the dematerialization of the potential significate of the noun[11] as a result of which we see the noun significate evolving away from its concrete senses towards an ever more abstract notional sense. We may now describe this evolutive dematerialization as a gradual widening of the horizon of the *import*, or, to use Guillaume's terminology, an increase in the extensivity of the potential significate of the noun.[12]

When, for example, in the vernaculars of primitive Indo-European the noun is felt to be close to its concrete senses, the extensivity of the potential significate is but little developed and the general and particular senses are not widely distinct. We may represent this as in Figure III.4.

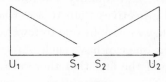

Figure III.4

11   See above, Chapter II.
12   This must not be confused with *extension* of meaning: extension concerns range of quantity and refers to amount included in the significate (external view); extensivity is a range of quality and refers to the extent of dematerialization of the significate (internal view). To include *wolf* in the notion of *dog* is to enlarge its extension, but not necessarily its extensivity. To evolve from *dog* a more abstract notion of *doggishness* is to enlarge the extensivity but not necessarily the extension.

In a highly evolved vernacular, on the other hand, where the noun is capable of great extensivity, this is due to the ever widening horizon of the universal which makes possible an ever more general grasp of reality (see Figure III.5).

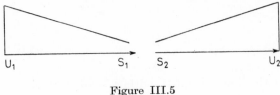

Figure III.5

Guillaume conceives of the operative mind (la pensée pensante) as "scanning" such mechanisms and systems in the act of representation and thereby arriving at a particular position:

Le mécanisme auquel obéit en l'espèce l'esprit humain est celui d'une *longitude* opérative, constructrice, et de *latitudes* résultatives marquant l'état d'avancement de l'opération constructive engagée et developpée en longitude.[13]

A chacune des coupes interceptives portées par le travers du mouvement ... correspond un 'effet de sens' momentané ...[14]

B. RELATIONSHIP OF ADJECTIVE AND NOUN

Because of the effects of the interplay between adjective and noun, and because of the quasi-substantivization of the adjective in such forms as *the poor, the weak, the lame,* it becomes necessary to say a word on the functioning of the adjective. Jespersen, who had many interesting insights on syntax, calls the noun a primary, the adjective a secondary and the adverb a tertiary.[15] This basic intuition, as we shall see, is very sound, but knowing the difficulties of talking about "substance" and "quality", he finds it difficult to talk any more exactly about nouns and adjectives than to say that "substantives are more special than adjectives, they are applicable to fewer objects than adjectives".[16] When it was objected that one can have such phrases as *a pink-eyed cat* and *a ten-roomed house,* in spite of the fact that there are more cats than pink-eyed beings, he can only say, "This, however, does not seem to me to invalidate the general truth of the theory as here explained: it must be remembered also that the real adjectival part of such combinations is *pink* or *ten*, respectively."[17] In

---

13 *Langage et Science du langage,* p. 186.
14 *Op. cit.,* p. 150.
15 Jespersen, *Philosophy of Grammar,* p. 96.
16 *Ibid.,* p. 75.
17 *Ibid.,* p. 80

Guillaumian terms the distinction between these three parts of speech is as follows: the noun has internal incidence, the adjective has external incidence of the first degree, and the adverb has external incidence of the second degree. Incidence means here the resting of an *import* upon a *support*, or the relationship between the carried and the carrier, the borne and the bearer. In the phrase *a very beautiful house*, for example, the words *very*, *beautiful* and *house* each carry a certain signification. *Very* carries its signification to *beautiful*, which thus becomes the momentary support or carrier of the notion of *very;* *beautiful* carries its signification to *house* which in turn becomes the momentary support or carrier of the notion of *beautiful*. But the notion of *house* does not require an outside support, it has its own internal support, and *house* thus becomes here a notion that can only be said of itself; the notion is here 'substantial' (see page 43) and brings with it its own support or bearer. This is, in fact what distinguishes the adjective from the noun: in the noun the incidence of the *import* upon the *support*, the relationship of the bearer of the notion to the notion borne, is internal;[18] the adjective, on the other hand, must have an external support for the notion it carries. There are thus three degrees of incidence which may be put in schematical form (Figure III.6).

IMMANENCE	TRANSCENDENCE$_1$	TRANSCENDENCE$_2$
HOUSE	BEAUTIFUL	VERY
internal	external	external
incidence	incidence	incidence
	in the	in the
	first	second
	degree	degree
(NOUN)	(ADJECTIVE)	(ADVERB)

Figure III.6

1) The noun has a notional import which has its own internal support (internal incidence).
2) The adjective has a notional import which requires a support elsewhere (external incidence of the first degree).
3) The adverb has a notional import which requires a support that itself has a support elsewhere (external incidence in the second degree).

The adjective in English may be substantivized, *i.e.*, used in place of a genuine noun: *the true, the beautiful, the rich, the poor*. These substantivized ad-

---

[18] Jespersen, *Philosophy of Grammar*, p. 80: "Only in rare cases will it be possible by heaping adjective on adjective to arrive at a complete definition of the notion evoked by the naming of a substantive: there will always, as Bertelsen remarks, remain an indefinable x, a kernel which may be thought of as the "bearer" (sic !) of the qualities that we have specified."

jectives, when used without further modification have always a generic sense. This is remarkable since, in Old English and early Middle English the combination *article + weak adjective* could have a particular reference:

þa dysigan = the foolish ones (the five foolish virgins)
þa gleawan = the wise ones (the five wise virgins)

When the morphology of the adjective was levelled to one invariable form in late Middle English, the prop-word *one* began to appear regularly for all particular references, and the substantivized adjective, by itself, came regularly to represent a full generic sense.

The levelling of the adjective morphology is interesting. Morphology does not normally disappear when it is needed; where it is an archaism it will tend to disappear, given the chance, or be remade, as was the morphology of the noun in Middle English, where almost all the old Germanic plurals and genitives were swept away under the levelling influence of final *s*. But the new morphology of the adjective was invariable, which suggests that the adjective in English had by this time been reduced to a simple transcendental function. (The adverb likewise does not vary according to the word it modifies.) The notion of *beautiful* does not have a singular or a plural; it is a formless continuate, and reflects the continuate usage of the noun which, while syntactically singular, is not the type of singular from which one can form a plural. Only a unit reference can be the basis from which a plural may be formed.[19] It is also remarkable that noun lexemes, when used as adjectives, are reduced to the continuate singular *(i.e.,* amorphous sense):

a footstool   = a stool for the feet
a toothbrush = a brush for the teeth
eyeglasses   = glasses for the eyes
ear muffs   = muffs for the ears

It is remarkable to what lengths speakers will go to obtain an unambiguously singular form. Firth speaks of "two of my phonetic colleagues",[20] thus preferring to use the adjective in an unusual extension of the sense rather than employ the noun form with its potentially ambiguous final *s: phonetics*. Compare, for example:

Two of my chemistry colleagues
Two of my chemical colleagues

In these two expressions the basic meaning may be stated as follows:

Two of my colleagues in chemistry
Two of my colleagues who are chemical

[19] *Cf.* above the list of non-numerical nouns: toast, advice, machinery, luggage, luck, fun, etc., which refuse all unit or plural reference.
[20] J. R. Firth, *Papers in Linguistics, 1934—51* (London 1957), p. 18.

As a result of the continuate, amorphous force of the adjective, reflected in its invariable form, English cannot use a substantivized adjective in a singular particular sense, nor in a genuine plural as may those languages where the morphology of the adjective is similar to that of the noun:

> un pauvre, ein Armer
> le pauvre, der Arme
> des pauvres, einige Armen

It is impossible to say in English *a poor, *(some) poors.[21] But, it will be objected, *the poor* in English is obviously and definitely a plural, since we say:

> The poor are to be pitied.

If, however, we consider the two following sentences:

> The beautiful was much discussed by Plato.
> The beautiful were envied by the ugly.

we observe that *the beautiful* may be either singular or plural, and we observe the resemblance to a state of affairs that will be discussed below (p. 62):

> The board has decided.
> The board have decided.

In these examples the agreement of the verb is dependent upon the *saisi*, that is to say, upon the situational content of the actual significate. *The beautiful* means *all that which is beautiful*, and like the word *all* itself, may be considered as a singular or plural depending on the *saisi*. Not having a final *s* it must be considered morphologically a singular, but if there is in the *saisi* the notion of a plural, a plural verb will follow, and our substantivized adjective may be considered as yet another example of the internal plural.[22] It is a mistake, therefore, but an understandable one, to talk as Mustanoja does, about the "survival of the plural adjective".[23]

The substantivized adjective is an adjectival notion to which no external support is given and the import of the adjective is therefore in search of a support. As a result it is forced to supply its own support, which may be obtained only from the total of the substantial elements to which it is normally attached: by attaching the notion of *beautiful* to that which has beauty, *good* to that which has goodness, *true* to that which has truth, *poor* to that which has poverty.

---

[21] Which is to say that while the notion remains adjectival it is impossible to make from it *a* or *some* particularities.
[22] See below pp. 61—63.
[23] Mustanoja, *op. cit.*, p. 645.

There are two ways of making a genuine substantive expression with the adjective. One way is called by Mustanoja (p. 643) "total conversion into a noun" as opposed to the partial conversion found in *the beautiful, the young.* In this case the adjective is remade as a noun with the total morphology of a noun:

>   an empty, the empties
>   a heathen, the heathens (also *the heathen*)
>   a sweet, the sweets
>   a native, the natives
>   a special, the specials
>   a dear, the dears
>   a savage, the savages
>   a modern, the moderns
>   a black, the blacks
>   a white, the whites
>   a regular, the regulars
>   a German, the Germans
>   a Christian, the Christians
>   a blank, the blanks
>   a Burgundy, some fine Burgundies
>   a western, westerns

The fact that certain adjectives may thus be recreated as nouns with a plural in *s* serves to underline the fact that the partially converted adjective is an amorphous non-numerical notion in which adjectival force is still felt, and that this amorphous significate arose in Middle English along with the loss of the adjective morphology common to Germanic.[24]

The second way of making a genuine substantive expression with the adjective is to add the prop-word *one(s)* or the noun *man/men: a young one, young ones, a poor man, poor men.* In colloquial discourse the unstressing of the propword *one* has led to the phonetic form [ðə jʌŋən] (the young 'un),[25] which would be identical to the objective form of the weak adjective had the latter survived.[26] It is also intriguing to observe that the weak adjective, according

[24] See Mustanoja, *op. cit.*, p. 644 (Although his conclusions may be questioned): "The remarkably free substantival use of the adjective in Old English and early Middle English in comparison with later times is doubtless largely due to the freedom allowed by the inflectional endings. Later in the ME period, when ambiguity following the loss of the inflections sets in, the semi-converted adjective has to give way to constructions where the adjective is followed by a noun or a noun equivalent. The alteration of *the innocent* in the Wyclifite Bible into *the innocent man* in the revised version is illuminative in this respect."

[25] The apostrophe in the normally offered spelling no doubt indicates absence of phonetic [w]. Is this neutralized pronoun the same element that occurs in the popular forms of the possessive pronouns: *hern, yourn, theirn, hisn* or are these made by analogy with *mine*? Or perhaps by analogy with *mine* because it has been wrongly analysed as *my'un*?

[26] Heinrichs, *Studien zum bestimmten Artikel*, p. 81, even goes as far as to say that the neutralized form of the pronoun in such expressions is a suffix. He offers no supporting evidence.

to Osthoff, Delbrück[27] and others was in origin a substantivized adjective (which later became again a genuine adjective) and that Prokosch says that in Early Germanic the compound character of the adjective stem and its suffixed element is "still quite distinct".[28]

The strong adjective declension of Germanic was the original Indo-European adjective that agreed with the noun. The weak adjective, it is generally agreed,[29] is a formation peculiar to the Germanic group,[30] made from the adjective stem with a suffixed substantive -n element that is an Indo-European ending used for marking animates:

> Latin: catus (sly) — Cato (the sly one)
> Greek: strabos (squinting) — strabōn (the squinter)

This new formation was normally placed after the noun at first:

> Strong — jungaz sunuz
> Weak   — sunuz jungo

Later it came to be placed in front, in the same position as the strong adjective. It has been suggested that because of its nominal force it was felt to be more of a noun in apposition than a genuine adjective[31] (hence its original position after the noun) and that later because of its adjectival stem it was felt to be an adjective of a different force and was therefore placed in front of the noun. This distinctive force was caused by the fact that it always had definite, never indefinite, reference, whereas the strong adjective could have either. As the system evolves, the weak adjective is utilized for definite reference, the strong adjective becomes reserved for indefinite reference. The weak adjective is almost invariably used with the definite article as this latter emerges, but occasionally, from the earliest texts until the disappearance of the adjective morphology in Middle English, the strong forms may be found with the article, and the weak adjective sometimes takes no article.[32]

---

[27] See Delbrück, "Das Schwache Adjektivum und der Artikel im Germanischen", *Indogermanische Forschungen XXVI* (1909), pp. 187—199.

[28] E. Prokosch, *A Comparative Germanic Grammar*, Linguistic Society of America (Baltimore 1938), p. 260.

[29] By Osthoff, Delbrück, Jespersen and Prokosch. Others (Hirt, Heinrichs, Mustanoja) assume that the ending is an added demonstrative (en/on); Prokosch comments that "this seems quite plausible, but it is hardly possible to prove it."

[30] A separate adjective declension is found in Old Slavic with a pronominal ending, but the usage is different.

[31] "*Haraldr unge* signifie donc étymologiquement 'Harald le jeune homme'." A. Meillet, *Caractères générales des langues germaniques*, 4th ed. (Paris, 1930), p. 184.

[32] See Christophersen, *The Articles*, pp. 102ff; O. Funke, "On the Use of the Attributive Adjective in OE Prose and Early ME", *English Studies* XXX, 1949, pp. 151—6; and Mustanoja, *op. cit.*, p. 233.

What was the special force of these weak forms? Jespersen comments[33] that the weak forms are "more special" than the strong forms even today in German. He also notes: " . . . we have a great many substantivised adjectives, but their meaning is always more special than that of the corresponding adjectives."[34] This is due to the transcendental nature of the genuine adjective, the fact that it may be used more widely than the noun; it is not limited by a support of signification but may in fact be attributed to things to which it does not genuinely 'belong': *a faithful replica*.

The noun, on the other hand, even when used as an adjective, carries with it a substantial, restrictive, immanent element. We may perhaps get some idea of the difference between strong and weak in Early Germanic by adding the substantial element *one* to the corresponding English adjective:

> jungaz sunuz — young son
> sunuz jungo — son young one

When the need arises in Early Germanic for distinguishing definite and indefinite reference, there is the means for developing, before the rise of the article, a crude system as follows:

> Definite — young one son
> Indefinite — young son

The articles, when they are fully developed, will make the distinction of strong and weak largely redundant, hence the disappearance of the old system in Middle English.[35]

Why should the substantivized adjective be incapable of carrying an indefinite reference? The answer lies in the differing relationships to the noun required of the normal (strong) adjective and the substantivized (weak) adjective. The strong adjective, as its varying agreement shows, has a temporary attachment sufficient for the exigencies of discourse — the import of the adjective is brought to bear directly upon the support of the noun it modifies; the attachment is not considered permanent and the import of the adjective is in fact removable or transferable. In the case of the substantivized adjective the import of the adjective is brought to bear first of all upon its own substantial element, which is then identified with the noun, and the notion is thus felt to be totally attached to the noun.[36] This can still be felt in Modern English in those cases where the adjective is substantivized after a proper noun:

---

[33] Jespersen, *Philosophy of Grammar*, p. 77
[34] Jespersen, *op. cit.*, p. 76.
[35] My own son, at the age of two and a half years, said "Red one book" for "The red book"; this was before he had learned how to handle the article system of English.
[36] The substantial element given the adjective is identified with the substantial element of the noun.

Charles the Bold, Frederick the Great, Jerusalem the Golden, America the Free.
Jungo sunuz can thus only have a referential or anaphoric force since it means
son to whom notion of young is totally attached (as a part of his 'substance'), and
this usage is feasible when we know of the son in question, whereas the normal
adjective is quite free from any such restrictions; similarly it is impossible to
say **America a Free, *Charles un Téméraire, *Friedrich ein Grosser*. The strong
adjective combination means, therefore, *young son;* the weak adjective
combination carries with it the force of *son that is known to be young* and therefore becomes suitable for expressing definite *(i.e.,* anaphoric) reference. When
this suitability is utilised the strong adjective becomes reserved for indefinite
reference and the pair form a contrasting system.

That this is not the sole or original aspect of the strong/weak contrast is
shown by the occurrences of irregularities of usage with the definite article
(þes ilces ȝeares, þes aþeles kinges) and the force of the contrast in certain
special terms, such as Old English *ān* = one. Declined strong it means *a*
certain; declined weak it means *alone* (= all one); the object thus modified
has the notion of oneness totally identified with it; it is all, totally one. Also
remarkable is the fact that *oþer* (other of two) is never declined weak.[37] It is,
of course, a notion that can be only accidentally attached for the purposes of
the moment; one can never be totally other. Even in Modern English we may,
as we have seen, substantivize other adjectives attached to proper nouns:
John the young, John the first, John the poor, John the faithful, but never *John*
the other. Since *the one* and *the other* are interchangeable, the substantial element
given to *other* can never be identified with any one person; as a result, we find
that *oþer* is always declined strong *(i.e,* temporary attachment). Similarly ·
one (ān) as opposed to *other* is always strong, the weak form being reserved for
the meaning *alone,* where there is identification of *oneness* with the person so
indicated.

The origin and, for the most part, survival of this simple mechanism may be
considered as typical of the Germanic group. Each group of languages has
certain phonetic tendencies; likewise it has certain grammatical tendencies and
other general tendencies in the means of expression. The use of prepositional/
adverbial particles *(e.g.,* up, off, out, on) conserved in the Germanic group
from an Indo-European pattern[38] marks a tendency to reserve a means of
clarification for use in discourse, that is, in the sentence. Likewise the creation
of a whole declension that substantivizes the adjective marks a tendency toward
the creation of concrete notions in discourse (by making the adjectival import

---

[37] The comparatives of ancient Germanic on the other hand were always declined weak
and may be compared in this respect with Greek comparatives in — $\iota\omega\nu$, — $\iota o\nu o\varsigma$, where
the same *-n* element appears. See also Meillet, *op. cit.,* p. 184.
[38] *Cf.* Meillet, *op. cit.,* p. 189.

as substantial as that of the noun). A similar facet of this tendency is the creation of noun compounds: *apple pie, chicken legs, station bus, bus station, stage door canteen, Landarbeiter, Seestreitkräfte*. Yet another facet of this tendency is the positioning of the adjective in front of the noun so that the adjective in discourse becomes a part of the noun significate, thus momentarily creating a new concept in discourse; this, if repeated often enough may go on to be a concept in tongue; it is in this way that *black bird* has become *blackbird, high lands* has become *highlands, long boat* has become *longboat*. German, as is well known, goes to great lengths to keep the adjective or other modifiers in front of the noun.

The import of the adjective in English can have a force that varies from complete dematerialization of the adjective significate to a genuine demonstrative, restrictive impact. In between is the stage of what we might consider the normal epithet. These three basic positions can be illustrated in schematic form as in Figure III.7, but it must not be understood from such a diagram that they are the *only* positions.

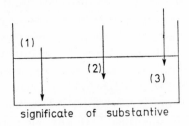

significate of substantive

Figure III.7

Examples of type 1:

The *old* boy came down in a rage.
Poor Max just stood there.

Examples of type 2:

A *cold* fury seized me.
The *delicate* aroma of oranges ...

Examples of type 3:

I said a *red* house, not a blue one.
Now that we live here, I often think of the *old* house.

There is a marked tendency in discourse to indicate these values of the adjective by the force of the stress. Adjectives of type 1 normally carry a weaker stress than the noun; adjectives of type 2 normally carry a stress equal to that of the noun; and adjectives of type 3 normally carry a stronger stress than that of the noun. But a word of caution is in order. In English only word stress can be said to belong to the level of tongue: a polysyllabic word, for example, has one particular primary stress, may have a secondary stress, and the other syllables may be considered to have tertiary stress:

‚desig′nation
‚inter′mittent
im′possible
a′bove
′beautifully
′recognizes
im‚possi′bility

This stressing is independent of the sense stressing found at the level of discourse in English. In sense stressing almost any word (or even syllable) in a sentence may be given extra stressing in order to display or emphasize it. In a sentence such as *That dog ran down our street* any one of the monosyllables may be given an extra force of stress to make it more prominent; this is an elocution exercise of a type given to actors. In similar fashion a sentence such as *I said EXclude him, not INclude him* shows, in capital letters, syllables that would not normally be stressed. The word stress in each case lies on the syllable *-clude*, but the first syllables are stressed here to underline the distinction sought for between the two verbs.

Sense stressing, which is fundamental to English, but unknown in some other languages (French, for example, which has no word stress either, but only phrase stress and occasional intensive stress), indicates a tendency already noted to reserve a means of clarification for use in discourse.[39] Word stress is fixed, but sense stressing is at the whim of the individual speaker and may, as we have seen, override the basic word stress. Sense stress, like word stress, has three basic levels: primary, secondary and tertiary. This complicates the question of stress when polysyllabic words are syntactically related: an adjective may have a stronger primary word stress than the primary word stress on the noun it precedes, due to receiving a stronger sense stress. This easily results in a confusion of these two quite different types of stress, a confusion that has already led to abortive attempts to describe the functioning of stress in English.[40] Sense stressing of the adjective is to be discussed in comparison with

---

[39] *Cf.* J. Orr, *Words and Sounds in English and French* (Oxford, 1953), p. 58: "The greater autonomy of the English individual word, which enables us by stress or by tone to throw into relief elements which, normally, are semantically insignificant, is in sharp contrast with the prevailing economy of the French sentence, in which, characteristically, the particular is submerged in the general."

[40] See A. A. Hill, *An Introduction to Linguistic Structures* (New York, 1958), pp. 13—30 and 102—105. See also discussion of Hill's approach in *Canadian Journal of Linguistics*, Vol. 4, No. 2, pp. 61—2; Vol. 5, No. 1, pp. 8—16; and Vol. 5, No. 2, pp. 77—80.

the primary stress of the following noun:[41]

> Stage one: weaker stress on adjective primary.
> *Old John.* (Familiar, may be said of a child)
> Stage two: equal stress on both primaries.
> *Old John.* (He really *is* old)
> Stage three: stronger on adjective primary.
> *Old John.* (Not young John)

It must be observed that while this basic patterning is generally followed quite faithfully, disturbances may occur due to the fact that it is a system at the level of discourse and is therefore not to be considered rigid. An extra force of emphasis on the noun itself, for any reason whatever, may change the whole pattern.

Just as the adjective can be a quasi-substantive, it may also be a quasi-adverb, having somewhat the function of an adverb while still operating as an adjective; this raises the whole thorny question of attributes, which may be of varying kinds; adjectives, nouns, prepositional phrases, participles, infinitives, adverbs. We normally think of the attribute as being opposed to the epithet because it is joined to the noun by a so-called copula verb:

> This is an empty bottle (epithet)
> This bottle is empty (attribute)

It is of note, however, that whenever the adjective goes *after* the noun in English it has similar force to the attribute:

> He left an empty bottle (epithet)
> He left a bottle empty (attribute)

The attribute positions fulfil the purpose of separating the adjective significate from that of the noun. We have seen[42] that the preposed adjective varies in force according to the degree of its penetration of the noun significate; the attribute adjective does not penetrate at all — it remains aloof from the noun significate in simple juxtaposition (see Figure III.8). The epithet adjective

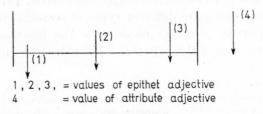

1 , 2 , 3 , = values of epithet adjective
4   = value of attribute adjective

Figure III.8

---

[41] Examples given here are all monosyllabic so that sense stress can be demonstrated without confusion with word stress.
[42] See above, p. 58.

becomes a part of the actual significate of the noun, creating a new concept in discourse; the attribute adjective does not become a part of the noun but remains a clear separate concept.[43] It develops connections with the verb as well as with the noun. Compare the following:

> He left the bottle empty.
> The bottle was left empty.

From the latter sentence emerges a verb *to leave empty*.

The epithet enters into the determination of the actual significate of the noun; the attribute arises after this significate has been determined. The effect of the epithet is to produce a single, total concept:

> quiet children
> open window
> empty bottle

The effect of the attribute is to produce a concept subjected to certain conditions *(i.e.,* two concepts):

> children quiet
> window open
> bottle empty

There is much more to be said about the attribute, but it lies outside the range of the present study.

C. SINGULAR + PLURAL

We have in the noun a basic opposition of singular and plural; arithmetical number consists of 1, 2, 3, 4, 5, 6, . . . *n*, whereas in English, linguistic number consists simply of singular/plural.

Some languages form an internal plural[44] (by dividing) whereby the notion of plurality is contained *within* the notion of the singular; the fossilized remains of such a system can be seen in the dual of Greek and early Germanic, and in the numerals of Russian, where two, three and four command the genitive singular; five, six, seven, etc. the genitive plural. This peculiarity can be attributed to the fact that it is very difficult to sustain definite plurals of

---

[43] It is not surprising that French, with its suppression of elements not provided for in *tongue*, should choose the postposed position as the common one for the adjective (utilizing the preposed position to indicate a dematerialized adjectival significate). It is also natural that English, with its preference for fresh construction and clarification in *discourse*, should normally use a preposed adjective.

[44] The term is from Guillaume; see for example, "Logique constructive du système des articles", in *Français moderne*, Vol. XIII, 1945, pp. 207—229.

this type higher than four units of division,[45] so that speakers of such languages in unsophisticated cultures tend to think in terms of "one, two, three, four, many".[46]

The Indo-European languages, although there are these remnants of a morphological internal plural, regularly form an external plural by multiplying from the singular. This is the psychomechanism of linguistic number, given in diagram form by the familiar binary unit or *tenseur binaire radicale*[47]

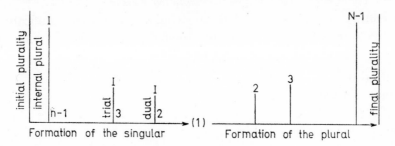

Figure III.9

(Figure III.9). The internal plural is contained in the formation of the singular, the external plural in the formation of the plural; the different stages represent the different values of each.

If in the internal plural the notion of plurality is contained *within* the notion of the singular, it follows that the form (or container) is felt to be singular, the matter (or content) to be plural. This is the case with such notions as occur in English;[48] the form of the lexical internal plural is always a singular: *a dozen, a few, a hundred*, but the matter or content is plural. In the external (grammatical) plural the plural is expressed in the *form*: in the case of English by the regular *-s* of the plural morphology. The distinction between the two types of plural is therefore as follows:

> Internal Plural = 1/N
> External Plural = N/1

Although there is no morphological internal plural in Modern English, there are some interesting usages of plural verbs with singular nouns when the *saisi* of the noun includes a plural notion:

---

[45]   Hence the vagueness of *a dozen people* as opposed to *twelve persons*.
[46]   These languages often have a complete noun morphology for *one, two, three* and *four*.
[47]   This figure is from Guillaume, "Logique constructive du système des articles", p. 210.
[48]   There are a handful of singular forms in English that have a plural notion in the significate, but there is, of course, no regular morphology of an internal plural in the noun: English does not have an internal plural, but an external plural.

The board have decided ...
The shoe department are having their sale next week.

and there is also the intriguing usage that has mesmerized the grammarians of the language: *a few men, a dozen eggs, a great many men.* Also to be considered as a related phenomenon is the indefinite *people*, singular in form,[49] but always treated as a plural:

Many people think ...
People are funny.

In similar fashion, when the form is plural but there is a dominant notion of the singular we may see singular verbs and singular agreements:

I have been saying that *this ten years*
Two hundred dollars *is* enough
A long five miles
A big twenty four inches high

D. NOTIONAL IDEATION AND STRUCTURAL IDEATION

It appears from these examples that verbs and adjectives may form an agreement with either the formal or material significate of the noun, with either the *container* or the *content*. The normal agreement, of course, is with the formal significate *(i.e.,* the container, the grammatical form[50]) but all these instances show that the force of the material significate may be such that the grammatical significate is ignored and the agreement made with the material significate *(i.e.,* the contents, the lexical element[51]).

The terms *content* and *container* are perhaps a useful analogy for the notions of material significate and formal significate, but they contain the misleading suggestion that these are two separate entities, whereas they constitute different, analytic aspects of one and the same thing: the significant. The terms *matter* and *form* may also mislead, since we have been accustomed to think of the matter as the meaning and the form merely the apparatus that conveys that meaning. In language, however, as in many other human affairs, both matter and form are *significant:* there is a difference of material significate between *man* and *fellow* since they occupy different positions in the lexicon, and a difference of formal significate between *man* and *men* since they occupy

---

[49] With its own external plural form: *peoples. Cf., They are a funny people.*
[50] The term *form* here has its Guillaumian sense of 'grammatical position'; it does not mean 'phonetic or graphic shape', or mere syntactic position.
[51] Guillaume on occasion used the term *semanteme* as a designation of the lexical element or material significate. See Guillaume, *Langage et Science du langage,* p. 99.

different grammatical positions in the grammatical architecture that is scanned in the generative processes.[52]

To accommodate these two aspects within the generative processes, Guillaume proposes that the act of representation contains a notional ideation which is followed by a structural ideation.[53] The notional ideation consists of the separating out of the particular notion which thus becomes opposed to all the others. The following structural ideation integrates this basic lexical content into the universalizing and interlocking forms of *number, function, part of speech*, etc. The total result is the production of the noun as a separate identifiable word at the threshold between tongue and discourse: potential significant (both materially and formally) as it arrives at the threshold, actual significant as it enters the act of expression (activity of discourse) the end product of which will be the sentence.

Although we have represented the structural ideation as following the notional ideation, it was Guillaume's opinion that, with the passage of evolutive time, the former tends to penetrate the latter and that this phenomenon is linked with the historical decay of the morphology of the noun declension in the Indo-European languages:

Quand cette naissance précoce de l'opération de discernement a atteint le maximum de la précocité possible, l'intervalle existant entre le début de l'opération de discernement et celui, consécutif, de l'opération d'entendement n'est plus que d'un instant, — au delà duquel les deux opérations deviennent coextensives et solidaires. Autrement dit à peine l'opération de discernement s'est-elle engagée que l'opération d'entendement s'engage en elle, dans la vue d'en infléchir du dedans, et le plus tôt possible, les effets.[54]

For the sake of simplicity, however, we shall represent these two phases of the act of representation as sequential (Figure III.10). This figure[55] applies here to English and is, in fact, valid only for Indo-European languages.

---

[52]   In building a frame house the difference between a 2×4 of spruce and a 2×4 of balsa is a material one. The difference between a spruce 2×4 and a spruce 2×8 is a structural one. The form and the material together constitute an indivisible unity in the world of experience but both aspects are individually significant to the builder.

[53]   He also used the terms *opération de discernement* (for the process which generates the semanteme) and *opération d'entendement* (which generates the grammatical form); see Guillaume, *Langage et Science du langage*, p. 100.

[54]   *Langage et Science du langage*, p. 100. The noun in modern French, for example, does not have the duality of stem + case marker (that was typical of Latin); material significate and formal significate are intertwined in a single morpheme.

[55]   *Cf.* R. Valin, *Petite Introduction*, pp. 71, 85, 86.

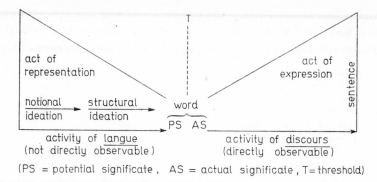

(PS = potential significate , AS = actual significate , T= threshold)

Figure III.10

E. DEMATERIALIZATION IN THE FORMAL SYSTEM OF THE NOUN

We have seen that the potential significate of the noun has varying extensivity not only from language to language, but also at different stages in the evolution of one and the same language: the potential significate of the noun in Latin is of restricted extensivity, hence the noun appears to remain close to its concrete senses; after twenty centuries of evolution the potential significate of the noun is, in Modern French, of wide extensivity, with a range that extends from the concrete to a state of pure notion.

We know that Classical Latin had difficulty in expressing abstract notions. It relied heavily on plurals to give a wider sense of extensivity, using thus a *discontinuum* (or sum of the total items) in order to reach a sufficient degree of abstraction:

> *Democritus, luminibus amissis, alba scilicet, et atra discernere non poterat.*[56]

In those languages that possess, through the process of dematerialization, a greater extensivity of the potential significate, the singular no longer retains the material notion of *a black thing, a white thing;* the material content has been stripped away and a resulting abstraction of the notions of white and black produced. Such languages may express these abstract notions with a singular or *continuum* (the singular extended without limit):

> *Democritus, after losing his sight, was in fact unable to distinguish between white and black.*

We have already noticed (p. 14) the remarkable process of dematerialization of the potential significate that has followed the evolution of the noun from Latin to Modern French and the fact that this dematerialization was accom-

[56]   Cicero, *Tusculan Disputations.*

panied by the loss of the Latin case system: Latin had five full working cases; Old French had two; Modern French has none. But history shows the noun shedding not only case, but all the morphological encumbrances of the Latin noun:

(a) case   tempus, temporis
(b) gender   taurus, bellum, mensa
(c) number   flos, flores
(d) declension portas, portus

The noun in Modern French has, in its phonetic form, lost almost all morphological expression of these four systems; gender and number are commonly expressed by means of the articles and other modifiers. The spelling retains the former sign of the plural but rarely a trace of gender.

There is an obvious relationship between the loss of these encumbrances in the noun and the development of an article system. Those languages that have kept alive a vigorous case system are precisely the ones that have developed no article (e.g., all the Slavic languages with the exception of Bulgarian). Expression of case in the morphology of the noun prevents the notion expressed by the noun from reaching general proportions: there is always a particular aspect of the noun expressed as well as the general notion — case tells us something about the *situation* as well as the *object* and thus adds an experiential element to the notion. Loss of case is therefore, by and in itself, a movement of desubstantiation.

It is possible that the different declensions of Latin are an archaic relic of a system of classifiers similar to those to be found in the Bantu languages of Africa; that the numbers of these classifiers (or groups) diminished with time (as is the tendency in Bantu) until a system of three (masculine, feminine and neuter, under the influence of the two fundamental animate and one inanimate types) was left along with the remains of the old system. These classifications are a means of representing entities that may be felt to be similar in form and to form similar groupings when there are more than one — in other words, expressions of linguistic number that take into account the nature of the thing viewed. This too constitutes a substantial or experiential element in the noun (as, for example, does the distinction of animate and inanimate in the Russian noun), linking the noun with the particular reality that it represents and thus hindering its development as a general notion. Elimination of declension and gender is also an evolutive step in the dematerialization of the potential significate.

In similar manner the expression of linguistic number in the noun supplies us, beside the notion itself, with information about the particular reality. With the elimination from the morphology of the French noun of the numerical substance inherent in the expression of linguistic number, the movement of dematerialization of the potential significate becomes complete; all that is left is the basic notion itself.

In his article, "Esquisse d'une théorie psychologique de la déclinaison",[57] Guillaume examines this state of affairs. He establishes that the *opération de discernement* or notional ideation of the noun is a movement of particularization, whereby a particular notion is discerned among the many that present themselves and that the *opération d'entendement* or structural ideation is a generalizing movement whereby the particular notion already established becomes a generalized part of speech, a noun (Figure III.11).

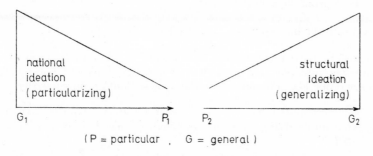

national
ideation
(particularizing)

structural
ideation
(generalizing)

G_1 P_1 P_2 G_2

(P = particular , G = general)

Figure III.11

If, however, the structural ideation begins precociously, it starts to underlie the notional ideation and generalise it before the genesis of the particular is complete:[58]

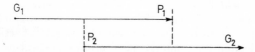

G_1 P_1

P_2 G_2

The result of the gradual penetration of the notional ideation by the structural ideation is then twofold: (1) the noun significate without some further definer, becomes incapable of representing a particularity and (2) the field of the structural ideation, previously freely available for the generation of the declension system, becomes restricted by the new involvement. The adjustments to this state of affairs are likewise twofold: (1) the genesis of an article system and (2) the necessity of expressing case by other means — whether syntactical position or preposition.

The generalized noun significate that results from this evolutive process is not suitable for most every day usage in discourse where there is constant

---

[57] In *Acta Linguistica*, vol. I, fasc. 3, Copenhagen (1939), reprinted in *Langage et Science du langage*, pp. 99—107.
[58] For the background of this figure see Guillaume, *Langage et Science du langage*, p. 101.

reference to particulars. Guillaume had already expressed this view in 1919:

Toutes ces étendues différentes, extrêmes et moyennes, sont incluses dans le nom . . .
Employer pleinement le nom serait les penser et les évoquer toutes d'un coup. C'est
trop, beaucoup trop pour le discours réel.[59]

He had also seen that the article system emerges as a solution to this problem
of representation:

Le fait que l'article est senti moins nécessaire lorsque la différence entre le nom dans
la langue et le nom dans le discours devient petite est de nature à suggérer l'idée
que l'article exprime cette différence.[60]

Twenty years later he expresses the same idea more forcefully:

le sémantème en arrive à disconvenir, dans l'immédiat, à toute application singulière
momentanée, n'étant plus dans l'esprit qu'une image purement notionnelle de concept, l'image d'une idée, non plus celle d'une chose dont on puisse parler.

Le problème est alors dans l'emploi du nom de lever cette disconvenance, de la
résoudre, selon qu'il est besoin, en la convenance utile. Il faut pour cela un signe:
qui est l'*article*.[61]

Later still (1944) he was to refine and clarify this basic insight:

Le nombre linguistique, celui qui fait partie de la flexion du nom, est porteur à lui
seul, dans les langues qui n'ont pas inventé l'article, du phénomène de l'extension
nominale. Possèdent l'article les langues où le phénomène de l'extension nominale se
scinde en deux parties: celle opérée selon le mode de la discontinuité, lequel, à tout
le moins du côté du pluriel, constitue le *proprium* de la catégorie du nombre et dont
cette dernière, en conséquence, ne saurait se dessaisir; et celle opérée selon le mode
de la continuité: cette seconde partie, de mieux en mieux distinguée, finit par s'ab-
straire de la première et se reporter sur un signe spécial, l'article, qui est dans la
langue le signe de l'extension nominale effectuée d'une manière continue.[62]

---

[59] Guillaume, *Problème de l'article*, p. 22.
[60] Guillaume, *op. cit.*, p. 21.
[61] Guillaume, *Langage et science du langage*, p. 106.
[62] Guillaume, "Particularisation et généralisation de l'article", *Français moderne*, tome
XII (1944), p. 106. (Article reprinted in *Langage et science du langage*, 143—156; quotation
is on p. 155).

IV

THE THEORY OF THE ARTICLE SYSTEM

A. DEFINITE AND INDEFINITE

In the early stages of the development of article systems the definite article contrasts with article zero; the indefinite article is regularly a secondary creation. There is a good reason for this.

There is more than one mechanism functioning within the structural ideation of the noun. If a semanteme is to become a noun, for example, it must be structured as having dimension, *i.e.*, as having a 'support-of-sense' for the basic notion or import. The relationship between support and import is, as we have seen, binary: the particularizing movement from the import towards the support we shall call the *objective presentation;* the generalizing movement from the support to the import we shall call the *subjective presentation*[1] (see Figure IV.1).

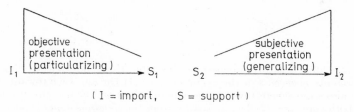

(I = import,   S = support)

Figure IV.1

When the notional ideation is allowed to complete its movement of particularization the import that is fed into the subsequent structural ideation of the noun is already particularized and suitable for particular reference; the particularizing movement of the objective presentation and the generalizing movement of the subjective presentation will not greatly affect it.[2] But as the

---

[1] *Objective* and *subjective* are used here in a technical sense.
[2] This state of affairs is still valid for the proper noun in Modern English, since its import is inevitably particular.

system evolves and the notional ideation becomes interrupted by the onset of the structural ideation, the import fed into the system is more generalized and the extensivity between the import and its support is widened. As a result, the particularizing movement of the objective presentation offers a quite different representation from that of the generalizing movement of the subjective presentation.

In the objective presentation the approach to the *terminus ad quem* (the particular and singular) and the particularizing approach from the general to the particular both combine to throw the total emphasis on the particular and singular; in the subjective presentation, however, the emphasis may be either upon the approach to the general and universal on the one hand or upon the term of emphasis, the *terminus a quo* (located with the particular and singular) on the other hand (see Figure IV.2). As the extensivity of the noun significate

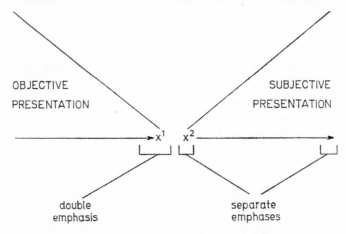

Figure IV.2. Differences of emphasis in the subjective and objective presentations. x^1 is the *terminus ad quem*. x^2 is the *terminus a quo*. (1) The approach towards the *terminus ad quem* is also a movement towards the support-of-sense. The movement and its term of emphasis both converge. (2) The departure from the *terminus a quo* is also a movement towards the import-of-sense. The movement and its term of emphasis diverge.

widens, the difference between the two possible emphases of the subjective presentation will become accentuated, whereas the combined emphasis of the objective presentation will be less immediately affected.[3] As a result, a demonstrative becomes necessary for those subjective presentations where a particular sense is intended, to distinguish them from those where a general or universal sense is intended. This demonstrative eventually becomes essential for all particular subjective reference and, accompanied by phonetic attrition

[3] This essential difference between the subjective and objective presentations finds its reflection elsewhere, notably in the fact that the indefinite article is used only with singular nouns, whereas the definite is to be found with both singular and plural nouns.

of the sign, develops into the definite article; but at this early stage it still keeps a great deal of its original demonstrative force. Such is the state of affairs in Old English and Early Middle English.

The next stage of development is a result of the confusion between the two very different types of zero article: the objective presentation with its emphasis on the singular and particular, and the subjective generic.

One solution to this clash is that of Classical Greek: to use the article with *all* subjective reference, even with proper nouns (see Figure IV.3). With such a system an indefinite article will only appear when the widening of the extensivity of the noun in tongue produces a clash between the general and particular senses of both objective and subjective presentations: Modern Greek uses ἕνας, μια, ἕνα as an indefinite article.[4]

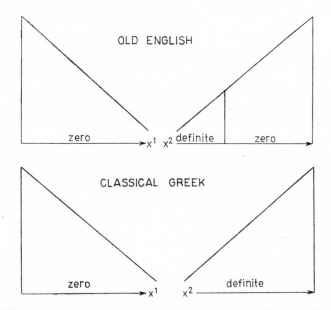

Figure IV.3. Historical stages of development showing the evolution of article systems.

Another solution is that of English: to use an objective definer to identify and emphasize objective reference; in late Old English and early Middle English both *an* and *sum* were used, the former eventually replacing the latter.[5]

---

[4] "Cette création d'un deuxième article est un fait important dans l'histoire des langues. Le moment qu'elle marque est celui ou toutes les représentations momentanées du discours — les subjectives comme les objectives — entrent en opposition dans l'esprit avec l'idée générale permanente du nom." (Guillaume, *Problème de l'article*, p. 17).

[5] See above, p. 21.

Once this contrast of article zero and the indefinite article is established, the indefinite proceeds in the same way as the definite article to expand its use to include the noun used in a more general sense, until it too may be used of a particular item:

> *A table* stands in the far corner of the room

or of a generalization:

> *A table* is a useful article of furniture.

This parallelism of usage between definite and indefinite articles attests a fully developed article system at the level of tongue: there is a choice of one or the other of the two articles and each, when accompanying the noun, is capable of expressing a wide range of extensivity from the general to the particular.

The speaker's choice of indefinite or definite reflects the basic contrast within the article system; it is obvious that the system reflects the binary character of the noun significate and shares the binary nature of so many systems at the level of tongue. We must not be content to view this binary unit as something static, or to view tongue as a bundle of such oppositions. For a word to arrive at the threshold of discourse from the depths of the unconscious mind, constructive processes are involved at the level of tongue, processes that are the activity of tongue, and this binary unit can best be expressed in terms of such a constructive process.

We have seen that the expression of a constitutive binarity requires the relationship to be stated twice, the second statement being the inverse of the first. Following this pattern, it can be seen that the indefinite article, being (a) introductory by nature and (b) related to the singular, is the sign of the approach from the general or universal to the singular or particular. Inversely, the definite article, being anaphoric (*i.e.* referential) by nature, is the sign of a movement that ranges from the singular already established to a second general or universal (Figure IV.4). There is an infinity of points along this continuous movement from U_1 through S_1 and S_2 to U_2; these points represent the infinity of possible uses in discourse. This binary figure is a complete and single statement of all the possible values to be found in the article system. We may suppose that the mind of the speaker, involved in the constructive processes of

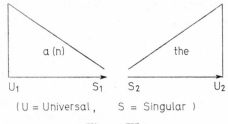

(U = Universal ,   S = Singular)

Figure IV.4

tongue, scans the system and adopts the position that is momentarily suitable for the representation sought.

The value of the different positions throughout the system can be most easily demonstrated by giving examples for the four cardinal positions:

U_1 — A table is a useful article of furniture. (general)
S_1 — A table stands in the corner of the room. (particular)
S_2 — The table stand in the corner of the room. (particular)
U_2 — The table is a useful article of furniture. (general)

Guillaume points out that each position adopted has both a kinetic and a static value. The kinetic values of the indefinite are all oriented toward the particular and singular; those of the definite towards the general and universal. Position will decide the scope of the idea as presented (general-particular), the movement determines the aspect under which the idea is viewed (approach-withdrawal). In this way the generalization to be found in position U_2 is a more complete generalization since it is general not only by position but also kinetically, since the movement involved is oriented from the particular to the general; whereas the generalization to be found in position U_1, although by position general in scope, is oriented kinetically toward the singular and particular. The nuance is a fine one, but it can be seen that the speaker, when using

(i) *A table is a useful article of furniture*

commonly has in mind a single table that serves as the basis of his generalization. In the context of situation where

(ii) *The table is a useful article of furniture*

would be used, such a factor would not normally enter the frame of reference. In other words (i) contains in its perspective a typical representative example; in (ii) on the other hand the movement of thought itself is directed toward the universal and general.[6]

The article *a(n)* represents at the level of tongue a refining movement from the general to the particular, from the universal to the singular: the dominant element in all its values will be this movement. It is a sign of presentation, of introduction, of refinement, of clarification, of approach to a more definite grasp of the notion. When we say, in position U_1

A table is a useful article of furniture

Cf. Guillaume, "Particularisation et généralisation dans le système des articles français", in *Français moderne*, Vol. XII (1944), esp. pp. 99—105.

it is not *just one table* that is referred to, although a particular instance may serve as a basis for the generic statement. But when we say, in position S_1:

> *A table stands in the corner of the room*

the movement of refinement has reached its term and the reference is to one, and only one, particular instance.

There is, of course, a multiplicity of values to be found in discourse between the two terms U_1 and S_1; all have in common this same aspect toward the singular and particular. Except in those rare instances we have noted, where a singular form clashes with its plural content,[7]

> *a dozen eggs, a few men*

the indefinite article is not used with plurals.

The opposing notion to *introduction* is *recall;* the definite article is a sign of recall. Having introduced *a table* the speaker may then refer to it as *the table;* it is not possible to introduce it as *the table* and then refer to the same article in the sense of a particular instance as *a table*. Compare the following:

> 1) A table stands in the corner of my room
> 2) The table was given to me by my father

(where the mechanism of recall is functioning), with:

> 1) The table stands in the corner of my room
> 2) A table was given to me by my father

(where the mechanism of recall is lacking). This interplay of the aspects oe introduction and recall is explained by the positions proposed for each articlf within the binary unit.[8]

Sapir *(Language,* pp. 85—86) enlarges on the subject of these two different values:

If *the* is omitted (farmer kills duckling, man takes chick), the sentence becomes impossible; it falls into no recognized formal pattern and the two subjects of discourse seem to hang incompletely in the void. We feel that there is no relation established between either of them and what is already in the minds of the speaker and his auditor. As soon as a *the* is put before the two nouns, we feel relieved. We know that the farmer and duckling which the sentence tells us about are the same farmer and duckling that we had been talking about or hearing about or thinking about some time before. If I meet a man who is not looking at and knows nothing about the farmer in question, I am likely to be stared at for my pains if I announce to him that 'the farmer (what farmer?) kills the duckling (didn't know he had any, whoever he is)'. If the fact nevertheless seems interesting enough to communicate, I should be compelled to speak of 'a farmer up my way' and of 'a duckling of his'. These little words, *the* and *a*, have the important function of establishing a definite or an indefinite reference.

---

[7] See above, p. 63.
[8] *Cf.* Guillaume, "La question de l'article", in *Français moderne*, Vol. XIII (1945), p. 80.

The indefinite article is not followed by plurals, but the definite article may be followed by singular and plural alike. Its movement is the reverse of the movement of refinement found in the indefinite; it is a movement of generalization, a movement of abstraction, of passing beyond the particular to the general and universal. This is the article that we use when making generic statements, statements about the *genus:*

The child is father to the man.

It allows us to go beyond or transcend the basic instance and thus get a more global, more general, more categorical, more abstract view; this, because it represents a movement of approach toward the universal, away from the singular and particular.

Since both articles can be used in referring to both the particular and general aspects of notions, only a principle of movement (which is the cornerstone of Guillaume's theories of psychomechanics of language) can explain the difference between the two. This can be seen very clearly in the distinction drawn between the two universal positions:

U_1 — *A table is a useful article of furniture*
U_2 — *The table is a useful article of furniture*

(as outlined above, pp. 72—74). The validity of the principle of movement can also be observed in the interplay of the aspects of introduction and recall:

(a) A table stands in the corner of my room
(b) The table was given to me by my father

These two movements represent the content of the articles, in so far as they may be said to have content. They have no material, only mechanical content,[9] which can only be represented schematically.[10] As well as the linear representation used above (Figure IV.4) we can represent these values by other figurative or formal means. The indefinite may be represented as a centripetal movement (Figure IV.5a), the definite article as a centrifugal movement (Figure IV.5b) in circles where the periphery represents the universal or general, the centre the singular and particular. This representation is useful for demonstrating the syntactical relationship between article and noun. If we represent the noun as a circle where the periphery reflects the universal sense of the potential significate, the centre the singular and particular sense of the potential significate, and then place in relief against it our figures of the articles, it can be seen that the movement which is the sole content of the articles begins to operate as a clarifier of the notion to which it is syntactically attached (Figure IV.6).

---

[9] *i.e.* they represent grammatical positions in the system of the noun.
[10] The schema will indicate their positions.

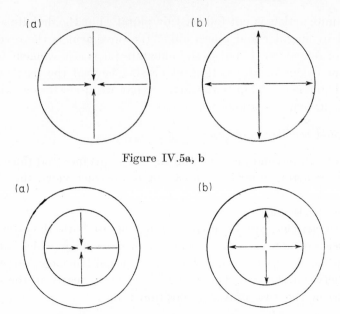

Figure IV.5a, b

Figure IV.6 (a) function of indefinite article, and (b) function of definite article.

B. THE ZERO ARTICLE

When the speaker wishes to use a noun to express in discourse a significate equal in scope to the potential significate, it is obvious that no article will be needed or used.[11] This is in fact the almost universal usage with the proper noun,[12] except in those cases where a restriction in the full sense is intended:

> *Shakespeare died in 1616.*
> *The young Shakespeare . . .*
> *The old Shakespeare . . .*
> *The Shakespeare of the sonnets . . .*

The bare unqualified noun (article zero) calls into play all the potential values together; in those cases where such an actual significate is sought for, the noun with article zero will be therefore satisfactory, but in cases where a more restricted sense is required, the articles or other definers will be used.

[11] "Cette tendance commune à ne pas mettre l'article devant les noms d'un certain type constitue un indice très net de la véritable nature de l'article en ce qu'elle démontre que les noms les plus sujets à s'en passer sont ceux qui comportent les moindres possibilités de variation durant le passage de l'idée générale, déposée dans le trésor de la langue, à l'idée plus réelle et moins générale, exigée par le discours." (Guillaume, *Problème de l'article*, p. 21).
[12] The exception is of course Greek; since zero was the 'sign' of the indefinite, the definite article became generalised for any anaphoric representation.

There is in fact a threshold between definite and indefinite usages on the one hand and zero usage on the other. This threshold is observed to shift with the shifting extensivity of the potential significate as the language evolves. When there is little difference between the universal and singular senses in the noun, both are satisfactorily expressed with zero article. Such a noun will lack any great degree of elasticity in the notion; this is the state of affairs in Classical Latin. When the extensivity begins to increase with the passage of time, the most concrete notions will require articles or definers, and the bare unqualified noun (article zero) will express a notion more general, more abstract than before. As the extensivity of the potential significate increases, so does the extensivity of the article as it encompasses further categories of expression.[13] This process can be seen taking place in the evolution of French; the different systems to be found in different centuries have been tabulated by Guillaume and the progressive use of the article to further and more general categories demonstrated.[14]

In Modern French all nouns except the names of people require an article or other definer unless the significate in view is felt to remain in the realm of pure notion, lacking any reality exterior to the mind; the article is, in this way, not only a definer, but also an instrument of *actualization*.[15] The threshold between use and non-use of article lies between the presentation of the notion as something real and its presentation as pure idea.[16]

In English the noun without article does not represent a mere idea, a total abstraction. It may represent, in fact, a concrete reality, but a reality without clarifying exterior form, a mass-word or continuate. Add an article and the concept is given form and becomes a thing-word or class-word; the threshold in English lies between the presentation of the notion as a formless, non-numerical entity, and its presentation as a separate singular entity, member of a class and necessarily having form.

The grammars distinguish between class words, which take the article, and mass words, which do not. If one is to understand by that that a mass word is a different word from a class word (or, to put it in other terms, that a non-numerical noun is different from a numerical noun) the distinction is false — a class word is merely the mass word defined and given form by the use of the article. It is obvious that

the oak expresses a concept that is numerical and has form — that of a tree — and is a concept that can be multiplied to form a plural;

[13] *Cf.* Mustanoja, *op. cit.*, pp. 230—231.
[14] Guillaume, *Problème de l'article*, pp. 67—87.
[15] Guillaume, *op. cit.*, p. 21.
[16] Guillaume reserves the term "article zéro" to those compounds *(perdre patience, parler politique)* that have a "homogénéité égale à celle d'un verbe fait d'un mot unique". See "Logique constructive du système des articles", pp. 225—229.

oak is non-numerical, is formless — it represents simply matter or material (in this case wood) and although syntactically it may take a singular agreement, it is not a singular that can be multiplied to form a plural, but rather a pre-singular or pre-numerical.

The following random selection will show that this is not a lone or unusual example, but that it represents a means of expression that is utilized to a considerable degree:

character, a character, cloth, a cloth, cake, a cake, dress, a dress, glass, a glass, hair, a hair, instruction, an instruction, land, a land, lead, a lead, grain, a grain, radio, a radio, straw, a straw, tin, a tin, verse, a verse, drawing, a drawing, song, a song, fight, a fight, carpet, a carpet, play, a play, night, a night, light, a light, chicken, a chicken, newspaper *(le papier journal)*, a newspaper *(un journal)*

Christophersen very sensibly points out that objections may be raised to the term *mass-word* for such abstract and intangible entities as *love* and *generosity*, and that it is hard for some people to grasp that *thing-words* may be non-material in sense. He proposes the excellent terminology *unit-word* and *continuate-word*, but never clarifies the terrible ambiguity of *word*. Although aware of the Saussurean and Guillaumian distinction between *nom en puissance*[17] and *nom en effet*,[18] the fact that unit-words and continuate-words are different usages of one and the same *nom en puissance* eludes him, however close he may come on occasion to perception and statement of the fact:

It was mentioned above that the same word may in one connection be a unit-word and in another a continuate-word. This is true of the list of words under the first diagram on page 24, and others may be added almost ad infinitum: *brick, coin, experience, feeling, fruit, hair, paper, stone, war*. Names of animals become continuate-words to designate the meat used as food: *fish, lamb, I like trout better than salmon;* and names of trees are continuate-words when they denote the wood or material: *a table made of oak.*

This, then, shows that the unit-words and continuate-words are not absolute groups but only represent different modes of apprehension. The transition of a word from one group to the other is an extremely common phenomenon.[19]

Christophersen's book is most interesting and is a big step forward from such views of the article as may be found in earlier writers:

It is sometimes said that such relatively insignificant words *(i.e.* as the articles) are grammatical tools. But the function of tools is to achieve some specific end. That is precisely what, in many cases, the article does not do, or at all events does only in a

---

[17]   *nom en puissance* = onymeme, or noun in tongue.
[18]   *nom en effet* = allonym, or noun in discourse.
[19]   Christophersen, *op. cit.*, pp. 26—27. Jespersen *(Philosophy of Grammar*, p. 200), however, sees that it is a question of one and the same word.

very slight and uncertain degree. Often it is mere useless ballast, a habit or mannerism accepted by an entire speaking community. The accumulation of old rubbish is so easy.[20]

Christophersen is also greatly influenced by Guillaume, but working only from *Le Problème de l'article* (1919), he does not get a full grasp of Guillaume's theories and of the ideas that are to be found only in germ in the 1919 book, and admits himself baffled by some of the obscurities to be found in it:

Guillaume's book is extremely interesting and fertile in fresh ideas which have profoundly influenced my own view; but it is neither quite clear nor quite consistent. His style and arrangement are wanting in perspicacity, and he is often so subtle that in spite of his wordiness and frequent repetitions of himself, I do not pretend to a full understanding of all his points.[21]

As a result there is no notion of a binary system in the article, nor of movement, activity, *energeia*, with its underlying *temps opératif*, nor of a monistic approach to the system of the noun, and only doubt and bewilderment concerning the relationship of the article system of French (or any other language) to that of English:

Basing our theory of the article exclusively on Guillaume's thesis, we can hardly get a consistent view of the English system. If one compares the systems found in the various Indo-European languages, they turn out to have so many common features that it is tempting to try to explain their differences as due to their representing different stages of the same historical development. It is unsatisfactory, to my mind, to look upon the English system as only an unfinished one and to measure it by a standard which is alien to it. Whatever may be its future, it is natural to look for a balance in the system itself, and it is clear that Guillaume's theory, as it stands, does not apply very well to modern English. It was devised principally for French, and, dealing with English, allowance will have to be made for the obvious difference between English and French on this point.[22]

I think it is totally wrong to conclude that Guillaume felt in 1919 that the different article systems represent "different stages of the same historical development". He does point out the similarities between the system of Old French and that of Modern English, and proceeds to demonstrate how the Old French system has evolved to its logical conclusion in Modern French. It does not necessarily follow, as Christophersen claims, that Guillaume "clearly regards it (the Modern English system) only as the French system in embryo". There is, in fact, evidence to the contrary; Guillaume sees the Modern French as *one* solution to the problem of the article; the problem is common to all those Indo-European languages that possess the article, but the solutions to

---

[20]   A. H. Gardiner, *The Theory of Speech and Language* (Oxford, 1932), p. 47.
[21]   Christophersen, *op. cit.*, p. 57.
[22]   Christophersen, *op. cit.*, pp. 66—67.

the problem differ, even though they show a tendency to evolve in similar fashion. The full title of Guillaume's book is *Le Problème de l'article et sa solution dans la langue française;* the full solution of the problem to be found in another language must be sought elsewhere, however similar the system may be in its appearance and evolution. This similarity of system is influenced by factors peculiar to each language, and is still only a *similarity*, which is not to be confused with *identity* of systems, nor *parallelism* of systems following an identical evolution at different rates. Guillaume states his intentions clearly on page 13 of his introduction:

L'ensemble des considérations qui précèdent règlent l'ordonnance du présent ouvrage. Les grandes tendances qui se correspondent dans les divers systèmes sont relevées succinctement dès cet avant-propos et fournissent la donnée première en vue d'une restitution du problème de l'article. L'étude se continue par un parallèle entre la solution-type exigée par le problème et les solutions réalisées successivement dans la langue française. Celle-ci a été retenue, par préférence, pour ses qualités d'exemple: elle renferme toute sorte de complications et se montre ainsi propre à faire échec aux hypothèses insuffisamment fondées.

It would seem from this that Christophersen, accustomed perhaps to a purely historical approach, has interpreted "Les grandes tendances qui se correspondent dans les divers systèmes" as "different stages of the same historical development" — an abusive interpretation. The problem is the same, but everywhere the situation is different, and requires a different solution.

The *nom en puissance* of French appears to be of greater extensivity than that of English. As a result the use of the article in discourse is far more frequent in French and the noun with no article or definer represents mere notion only, not imagined to have any equivalent exterior reality. The most extended senses of the *nom en puissance* of English, since it is of more restricted extensivity than its counterpart in French, still retain a certain concrete matter, so that a noun used with zero article may represent a concrete, though formless, reality. These simple facts lie behind most of the conflicting usages to be found in the two languages. The article is needed in French to represent even a formless, limitless entity, such as may be expressed in English by the bare noun: *le beurre = butter, la viande = meat.*

Why should the *nom en puissance* of French have reached more quickly to a state of greater extensivity than has its counterpart in English? I doubt if one should try to answer such a question, but one thing is sure, that the French article, being also a marker of number and gender, is also more necessary in discourse for clarity of expression than are the completely neutral *a(n)* and *the.* The continuous presence of the article, necessary for other, more practical purposes, frees the noun in its movement towards a greater extensivity, and since number is already expressed in the article, permits the extraction, from the noun, of the expression of numerical content. The result is, in French, a noun that in its phonetic form expresses neither number nor gender, both of which are expressed by a preceding article.[23]

This secondary usage of the article is not to be overlooked. One finds, for example, that the article is used in certain cases in German as a marker of case, where otherwise it could be left out. Compare the following examples:

Ich trinke lieber Bier als Wein.
Ich ziehe Bier dem Wein vor.

It is even used, for the same purpose, with proper nouns:

Socrates Leben.
Der Tod des Socrates.[24]

It is remarkable that a borderline usage, once instituted for any purpose whatever, may bring about a whole shift of system.[25] It follows that such usage as that above could easily precipitate a more generalized use of the article, accompanied by a shift towards a state of greater extensivity in the *nom en puissance*, just such a shift, in fact, as that which has taken place between Old French and Modern French.[26]

The fact that this secondary usage has been lacking in English since early in the Middle English period may well explain why the use of the article, since it is not necessary for the marking of number, gender or case, has not spread to a greater range of categories, in spite of the increase in the extensivity of the *nom en puissance*. The fact that the article is not necessary for these secondary purposes has also undoubtedly encouraged the growth and maturity of a zero article that in English has great force and range of expression.

Our analysis of the article system into a binary unit consisting of two movements, (an introductory movement of approach followed by an anaphoric movement of departure) may seem somewhat arbitrary unless it is pointed out that the other definers of English follow a similar pattern. To this

---

[23] Article and noun have evolved in French to a point where it may almost be said that the article is the *form* of the noun.

[24] Examples from Christophersen.

[25] "Au surplus, il faut se représenter que la *pression* sémantique s'exerçant sur tout le langage, lorsque celui-ci cède en quelque partie, les autres parties tendent à se mettre de niveau. En un temps plus ou moins long, il peut se produire ainsi des changements conceptuels non apparents, mais très profonds, qui sont la conséquence d'un léger accident." (Guillaume, *Problème de l'article*, p. 40).

[26] It might also be pointed out that the article is used more often in Modern German than in English, (see Jespersen, *Philosophy of Grammar*, p. 203) and that the usage in German approaches the usage in French. In this respect, therefore, German, according to Christophersen's understanding, would be more "advanced" than English, although not as advanced as French. This in spite of the fact that German, in its morphology and syntax, shows a remarkably more conservative face than does English: a fact that supports the contention that a different situation will require a different solution to the problem of the article.

end it may be of value to demonstrate the functioning of a system closely related to that of the articles: the system of the demonstratives *this, that, these, those.* We are accustomed to being informed by the grammarians that *this* represents that which is near, and is opposed to *that*, which is used to represent whatever is distant: "*This* and *these* refer to what is near in space, time or conception, *that* and *those* to what is further off."[27]

One might quite easily ask in what way such notions could be said to belong to a system of two movements, an introductory movement of approach followed by an anaphoric movement of withdrawal, a binary system that reflects the fundamental binary relationship of man and the universe[28] (see Figure IV.7).

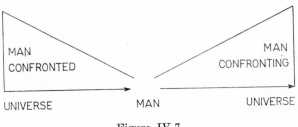

Figure IV.7

But a closer examination of the usage of *this* and *that* reveals some interesting facts: (1) "In some cases *this* refers to what is to follow, *that* to what precedes."[29] (2) "*This* and *that* may also refer to persons, *this is* being especially used as a formula of introduction or identification."[30] (3) Proximity and distance play no essential part in many usages. In the following pairs one or the other may be used in most situations, regardless of distance:

    a. Is this a table?
       Is that a table?
    b. This is true.
       That is true.
    c. This is one of his greatest paintings.
       That is one of his greatest paintings.

Nevertheless *this* and *that* have always a spatial or temporal reference. They can be used to refer to anything from the farthest dimensions of the universe (space/time) down to the *hic et nunc* (the here and now) of the individual consciousness. This is, in fact, the basis of the relationship of the general and the

---

[27]   Zandvoort, *A Handbook of English Grammar* (London, 1957), p. 147.
[28]   The idea of this figure is based on an unpublished manuscript of Guillaume.
[29]   Zandvoort, *op. cit.*, p. 148.
[30]   Zandvoort, *op. cit.*, p. 149.

particular that forms the binary system of the English demonstratives: *this* is the sign of an introductory movement of approach to the *hic et nunc; that* is the sign of an anaphoric withdrawal from the *hic et nunc.* (See Figure IV.8)

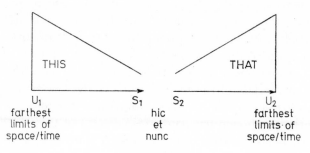

Figure IV.8

(i) The introductory sense of *this* is borne out by items (1) and (2) above. *This* is also used as an introductory element in the telling of anecdotes: "There was this Scotsman ..."

(ii) The anaphoric sense of *that* is supported by the evidence in (1) above. There is also the very frequent anaphoric use of *that* with following relative: *That which = The one which.*

(iii) The movement of approach suggests involvement; that of withdrawal suggests aloofness to the entity referred to. These emotional overtones play a great part in those usages where proximity and distance have no part in the expression, as in (3) above. No matter how near or how distant, either *this* or *that* will be used because of the *aspect* that it gives to the noun and the emotional overtones that accompany each aspect.

(iv) *This* is the term which may signify arrival at the *hic et nunc* and is therefore the obvious choice for expressing the *hic et nunc: this week, this place.* The aspect of *that* is always towards the elsewhere and other time. It is in fact the aspects of approach and withdrawal which decide usage, rather than whether a thing is near or distant. The aspect of approach will yield an impression of proximity; the aspect of withdrawal will yield one of distance in just the same way as these aspects suggest involvement and detachment.

(v) Regardless of distance, a man may be described as *this man* or *that man.* As he approaches, however, one can only sensibly call him *this man;* as he leaves, *that man.*[31]

(vi) Only a principle of movement will enable all the different values of *this* and *that* to be summed up under one simple mechanical system at the level of tongue.

[31] *Cf.* the schoolboy 'joke' about Stirling Moss (the famous racing driver): "Ladies and gentlemen, this is Stirling Moss, that was."

(vii) The plurals *these* and *those* follow the same systemic pattern as the singulars *this* and *that*.

(viii) It is interesting to note that the anaphoric demonstratives *that* and *those* have the same etymology as the definite article, also anaphoric by nature. *That* comes from the neuter singular nominative and accusative form of the Old English article: *þæt*. The unstressed forms of the Old English article became neutralized to *the* (see above, page 16); to arrive at a form *that* in Modern English we must presume a continuation of emphasis and stress on the word, which prevented the loss of the final consonant and the neutralization of the vowel, a neutralization which has been common to the unstressed syllables of English since the tenth century. The stressed form of the Old English article gives a modern demonstrative; the unstressed form evolves to become the modern article.

The nominative and accusative plural (all genders) of the Old English article is *þa*. Unstressed, the form becomes *the;* continually stressed, this same form would have evolved to *tho* in Modern English. (This form is to be found in Middle English and even occasionally in Early Modern English.) To this has been added, perhaps by analogy with *this* and *these*, the -*s* of the Germanic demonstrative forms to give us the composite form *those*.[32] *The, that* and *those* all stem from the Old English declension of the definite article.

The system of signs or semiology of a language will always tend to reflect, however imperfectly, the mental systems that lie behind the signs; conservatism and archaisms, reminiscent of former systems, will spoil the perfection of this reflection. In the forging of a new system, as in the creation of neologisms, the most convenient signs to hand will be the ones that will most often be used to cover the new significates; all semiology, though arbitrary, is formed from pre-existent materials. This principle can be seen functioning not only with the formation of the demonstratives and the definite article, but also in the formation of indefinite article *a(n)* from the use of the numeral *one* is unstressed positions in both Old and Middle English. *La sémiologie fait flèche de tout bois*.[33]

---

[32]　Karl Brunner, *Outline of Middle English Grammar* (Oxford, 1963), comments (p. 62) that the Middle English form *þas* is "a new formation probably derived from *þa* and the -*s* of noun plurals", and again (p. 63): "The form *those* is hardly a reflex of the long lost plural *þos* of the emphatic demonstrative . . ., but rather a new formation by analogy with the plural of the emphatic demonstrative *þese*." Whatever the provenance of the *s*, the form is clearly analogical.

[33]　Dictum of Guillaume.

V

THE INDEFINITE ARTICLE

A. EXTENSIVITY OF THE INDEFINITE ARTICLE

The indefinite article is an approach to the singular and particular. This movement of approach has a range that we have called the *extensivity* of the article; the extremes of this extensivity may be seen in our two examples:

U_1 — A table is a useful article of furniture.
S_1 — A table stands in the corner of the room.

These two different usages, representative of the two poles of the indefinite article, have been commented on by the grammarians:

The principal function of the indefinite article is to denote that we have to do with a single specimen of the class of persons, animals or things indicated by the noun (often with the implication that any other specimen of the class would have done just as well).[1] (Function S_1)

Sometimes the function of the indefinite article is rather to assign a person, animal or thing to a special class or kind.[2] (Function U_1)

Christophersen calls them the *individual use* and the *generic use*.[3] The difference between these two functions becomes more apparent when we convert instances of each into the plural as in the following examples:

i. There is a table over in the corner.
   There are some tables over in the corner.

ii. A bus stopped close to me.
    Some busses stopped close to me.

iii. He was reading a paper.
     He was reading some papers.

---

[1] Zandvoort, *A Handbook of English Grammar*, p. 124.
[2] Zandvoort, *op. cit.*, p. 125.
[3] In so doing he points out (p. 33) that the contrast between generic *a* and *the* is similar to that between *every* and *all*, a most interesting comment since these latter definers form a binary unit of total number in English. Space and subject matter forbid the demonstration of the fact.

The above examples are of Function S_1 and will be found to differ from the following examples of Function U_1:

  i. A table is a useful article of furniture.
    Tables are useful articles of furniture.

  ii. A hill is the opposite of a valley.
    Hills are the opposite of valleys.

  iii. A paper is not a luxury.
    Papers are not a luxury.

In Function S_1 it is perfectly natural to add the word *some* which continues the natural sense of the expression in the plural. *Some* cannot be added to the plural in the examples of Function U_1 without distorting the sense as intended in the singular. Since, however, these two different values represent the opposite poles of a continuous movement, we must expect other intermediate values which belong to neither function but to one of the many stages in between:

  We need a paper to support our cause.
  A paper appears every afternoon.

Süsskand, having made a careful and thorough investigation of a large number of texts, shows that the first usages of the indefinite article in its development were of a type S_1 and that the spread to the more and more generic senses was gradual.[4] This supports exactly the thesis that in its origins each article was of slight extensivity and that as the extensivity of the *nom en puissance* becomes enlarged with the evolution of the language, the extensivity of the article system is also enlarged to cover the gap arising between the newer dematerialized senses and the older more concrete senses. In other words, those senses which were, at one stage of the language, on the periphery of the *nom en puissance*, will at a later stage have been outstripped by the growth of the extensivity of the noun, and being, as a result, back from the periphery, will require an article to actualize them and distinguish them from the new, more dematerialised senses appearing on the expanded periphery of the *nom en puissance*.

We can observe this same evolution from the point of view of the article itself. The indefinite article is, in English as in all the other Indo-European languages that possess such an entity, of the same root as the numeral *one*. The genesis of an indefinite article may be said to date from the moment that the force of the numeral is lessened in any usage; it is in this way that a new version of the numeral — a dematerialized numeral — is produced, that will

---

[4] P. Süsskand, *Geschichte des unbestimmten Artikels im Alt- und Frühmittelenglischen*, *SEP* LXXXV (Halle, 1935).

eventually become a full indefinite article. Such uses are still reasonably frequent in Modern English:

> He emptied his glass at a draught.
> They were two of a kind.

From this usage it is an easy and natural step to include those cases where the reference is not just to *one and only one*, but to the single specimen mentioned by Zandvoort, that is, *one and any one*. This leads directly to a further widening of the extensivity and the use of the article to refer to *any one at all*, from which position it is a simple step to the generic use *every one*.

From the sense of *a specimen of a category* which is common to all these usages from the individual to the generic it would be easy to suppose that the use of the indefinite article has developed to such an extent because it is useful as a *classifier*. That it is a classifier in these usages there is no doubt, but the aspect of classification has been and is handled by other Indo-European languages without the intermedium of an indefinite article:

> Quid est? Est mensa.   (Latin)
> Shto eto? Eto stol.   (Russian)

What has caused the spread of the article is not that it is useful as a classifier, but that the *nom en puissance* has reached such a stage of extensivity that the indefinite article has become necessary, not only as a classifier, but also in any other usage that requires a representation of a single entity, individual or generic. We can, fortunately, still find in Modern English nouns that have but slight extensivity, and thus we may gain some insight into the operations of nouns of limited extensivity. Of such a type in Modern English are proper nouns belonging in common to more than one person: Mr. Jones, Mr. Smith. The relationship between the name and the person involved is felt to be very close, somewhat similar to the bond between word and thing in unevolved vernaculars and totally different from the relationship between the noun *table* and its potential significate. This fact has lead to endless debates among philosophers and others as to whether such a noun can be said to have connotation. Normally these nouns may be used without any article, it being assumed that, since the range of extensivity is slight, the person referred to is sufficiently clearly represented. But we may if we so wish add an indefinite article and say:

> A Mr. Jones called this morning.

It is remarkable that the value of this article is very similar to that found with the numeral *an* in Old English (see p. 13); it means *a certain Mr. Jones*. If we attempt to create a generic use of this same noun:

> A Mr. Jones would be a useful addition to any enterprise.

we may obtain a more abstract notion in the significate than that to be found in:

> A Mr. Jones called this morning.

but the reference is still singular, still limited to a certain Mr. Jones, and certainly does not include *every* Mr. Jones; it means "a man like Mr. Jones".
In similar fashion we may add the definite article to such a noun and say:

> The Mr. Jones called again today.

In view of the results obtained when using the indefinite article, it is not surprising that the value of the definite article is here, as frequently in Old English, very close to a demonstrative and could, in fact, be quite simply replaced by *that*.[5] Furthermore, any generic use with the definite article seems to be out of the question:

> *The Mr. Jones is a useful addition to any enterprise.

The only sensible way to make a generic statement without the use of *every* or *all* is by means of a plural, a means resorted to in similar fashion by Classical Latin (see above, p. 65).

> Mr. Joneses are indistinguishable from Mr. Smiths.

B. USE WITH PROPER NOUNS

It is useless to argue whether a proper noun has connotation or not. Some do, some do not, but all may.[6] Those that have no connotation have a one-to-one relationship with the significate in much the same way that a person's signature has with the individual so identified. Such a noun may develop, briefly or permanently, a wider extensivity:

> He is not a Mozart *(i.e.,* an exceptional musician).
> He is the Shakespeare of the twentieth century theatre
> *(i.e.,* its greatest dramatist).

But one may also find, in a usage that one might classify as personification, proper nouns where a famous name is *identified* with another person or type of person:

> Every great man nowadays has his disciples, and it is always Judas that writes the biography.   (Oscar Wilde)[7]

---

[5]   The analogy with Old English common noun usage is, of course, only partial, since the support-of-sense in a proper noun significate is, by definition, an invariable.
[6]   The mechanism is there to be used or ignored.
[7]   Qu. Jespersen, *Philosophy of Grammar*, p. 66.

There is a different sense here from the usage with the article. Unless this different sense is understood (it is similar to a nickname) this could be construed as an inconsistency in the use of the article; it is not — it is merely a stylistic trick of name calling. Such an instance, the different effect of which is immediately appreciable to those who speak the language, may also help us to appreciate unusual instances from Old English which are difficult to evaluate because to us it is a 'foreign' language.[8]

Apart from the great mass of common nouns to be found in any language of such wide propagation as English, there are (a) a fairly limited number of proper nouns that are common to most speakers of the language (names of continents and countries for example) and (b) an almost unlimited quantity of proper nouns of purely local and restricted use *(e.g.*, names of individuals and geographical landmarks). Nouns of category (a) will tend to have a limited extensivity, while those of category (b) will tend to have a one-to-one relationship with the significate, or at best an extensivity created momentarily for immediate purpose. It will be more common, therefore, to find nouns of category (a) requiring an article than instances of (b):

> The making of a new Canada
> We are opposed to the notion of a divided Germany.

Proper nouns may be distinguished as a separate subdivision of the noun; they are nouns just like any other nouns, except that their extensivity, for practical reasons, has not been developed. They form a continuum between the non-linguistic and the linguistic on the periphery of tongue. A noun that has developed no connotation, and therefore as a result no extensivity, no *repeatability* in other, different situations, has but little more claim to be linguistic than has a man's signature or his photograph.[9] But such a noun may develop an extensivity and become a common noun so that we find, among the group called proper nouns, a vast range of differing notions of varied extensivity; as a result they can only be described as a link, an endlessly shifting continuum between extralinguistic signs on the one hand and fully developed linguistic signs on the other.[10]

---

[8] *i.e.* No one today speaks it as his native tongue.

[9] These one-to-one relationships could be classified as instances of *code;* some such term is needed to distinguish such simple significations from the complex functionings of linguistic meaning. The common noun only has this one-to-one relationship when the significate is the word itself; we might call this the 'proper' usage of the common noun: He couldn't even spell *cat.* (Note that the convention of italics is similar to the convention of a capital letter with proper nouns !)

[10] *Cf.* Jespersen, *Philosophy of Grammar*, p. 69, "Linguistically it is utterly impossible to draw a sharp line of demarcation between proper names and common names", and p. 71 . . . "the difference being one of degree rather than kind."

C. INDEFINITE AS OPPOSED TO ZERO USAGE

The proper noun rarely requires or uses an article because it rarely presents less than its total potential significate; for this the bare noun is sufficient.[11] For a more limited representation an article will be necessary. In similar fashion, when the common noun is used to represent a formless continuate entity *(e.g. butter, generosity)*, it too does not require an article, the bare noun is sufficient.[12] When, however, there are restrictions, limitations or constrictions of the significate in view, as when the entity is seen with clear exterior form or is otherwise clarified from the vague, formless representation to be found at the limit of the extensivity of the *nom en puissance* (a representation that is satisfactorily presented by the bare noun), then an article will be called into play in order to achieve this more limited representation. This simple mechanism, as often happens, produces a variety of effects in discourse depending on the context and the noun affected. The following examples are quoted by Jespersen *(Modern English Grammar*, Vol. VII, pp. 432 ff):

> He was ready to do anyone a kindness.
> Sit down and have a drink.
> She had a fire in the parlour.
> Green vitriol is a salt.
> Imagine a shyness more powerful than curiosity or desire . . . .

In some of these usages the article is requisite; in others it is a stylistic suggestion; sometimes the zero form is the more unusual of the two:

> There was absolute silence.
> There was a short silence.

Kruisinga also quotes the following:

> What a difference to one's well-being is made by the possession of a comb.
> What difference I found between your words and mine.[13]

We may observe here a frequent effect provided by the contrast between the use of the article and article zero. The article introduces a unit reference, which gives an exterior, numerical view and therefore has overtones of quantity. The zero presentation, on the other hand, gives an internal, non-numerical view which has overtones of quality. These overtones are normal effects of internal and external views, regardless of the subject matter. Compare the following:

---

[11] See above, p. 76.
[12] See above, p. 8.
[13] Examples from Kruisinga, *Handbook*, Vol. II, p. 314.

External view	Internal view
(Container — quantitative)	(Contents — qualitative)

Fr. soir	= evening		soirée	= evening
Fr. an	= year		année	= year
Fr. matin	= morning		matinée	= morning
Fr. jour	= day		journée	= day

a verse	verse
a night	night

An internal view will reveal the contents, the principle aspect of which is type or quality; an external view will reveal the container, the principle aspect of which is size or quantity. We therefore tend to associate these aspects with these particular views. As a result it is natural to leave out the article with *absolute silence* and equally natural to add it in the phrase *a short silence*. In the other two sentences *What a difference* suggests quantity, whereas *What difference* suggests quality, and these overtones fit in exactly with the intended sense of the rest of the two sentences.

D. ARTICLE WITH ATTRIBUTES

The attributive use of the noun also causes some fluctuation in the use of the article, much of which has puzzled the grammarians. In certain cases it can safely be said that the word in question, although usually used as a noun, is unmistakably an adjective:

> She liked her servants to be Church of England.
> *(Cf.* Church of England servants)
>
> He was Science and I was Arts.
> *(Cf.* Science building, Arts building)
>
> I'm labour, he's communist.
> *(Cf.* a labour vote, a communist vote)[14]

In each of these three instances the predicated attributes *Church of England*, *Science*, *Arts*, and *labour* would make complete nonsense if allowed nominal force. Furthermore the adverb *very*, which is used as an intensifier only with adverbs and adjectives, may be added to each. In these instances the significate of the predicate itself prevents it from being felt with nominal force and causes it to be felt with adjectival force. Of a similar type are those cases where it is the notion inherent in the verb that prevents the predicate from having a

---

[14] Examples from Jespersen, *Modern English Grammar*, Vol. VII, p. 455.

nominal force. When a verb may be transitive, any following noun becomes a direct object; the predicate in such cases must therefore be given an adjectival, and avoid a nominal, force; this is done by omission of the article:

> He turned communist.
> *(Cf.* He turned green. He turned a corner.)

Because of this adjectival force, always present in the predicate attribute, many languages avoid an article with the attributive usage. In English, however, an article often *must* be used:

> He is a fool.
> My father was a soldier.
> He become a poet.

This article is used when the predicative noun is felt to classify the person concerned, that is, when it presents the notion of *a specimen of a category.* It is remarkable that resistance to this usage occurs when only one person may hold an office, position or rank mentioned in the predicate at one and the same time:

> I became a director. I became Managing Director.
> ... became Lord Mayor and a baronet.
> I was surgeon successively in two ships.[15]

In these cases the sense of *a specimen of a category* is lost and there is a one-to-one relationship between noun and significate similar to that found in a proper noun. Here the predicate noun refers to the title rather than to the person: *Prince of Wales* is a title, *a Prince of Wales* is a person; *Bishop of Durham* is a position, not a person, while *a Bishop of Durham* is a person, not a position. Many persons may hold the position, but the position itself has no plural. We are once again confronted with the contrast between unit usage (or numerical sense) and continuate usage (or non-numerical sense); unit usage requires the article, continuate usage, as elsewhere, uses the bare noun.

This continuate or non-numerical usage sometimes dominates where one might expect a unit usage, and the play between the two may be used for stylistic purposes:

> Marie was nineteen and virgin, but she was essentially woman.
> Now she was gypsy, pure gypsy.[16]

The presentation of the total range of the notion, achieved by the bare noun, is very close to the adjectival use noted above, the crucial difference lying in the

---

[15]   Examples from Jespersen, *Modern English Grammar*, Vol VII, pp. 451 and 453.
[16]   The qualitative force of zero reference is again remarkable and undoubtedly this is what is sought by the writer in instances such as these. The examples are from Jespersen, *Modern English Grammar*, Vol. VII, p. 455.

fact that in these cases an article may be used; in the adjectival use an article may never be used.

It is not surprising that the fluctuations of usage caused by the contrast of zero article (presenting the full range of the notion — qualitative overtones) and indefinite article (presenting a specimen — quantitative overtones), a contrast played upon with great delicacy by those who speak the language as a mother tongue (and who are therefore masters of the system), should have caused so much trouble not only to foreigners but also to the grammarians, who are always looking for *rules* instead of systems and thus tend to base unsatisfactory and frequently false statements upon the confronting (and conflicting) evidence. It is grossly wrong, for example, to state[17]

> We do not use 'a' or 'an' when the attribute is part of the object in an active sentence, and part of the subject in a passive sentence.

and quote as evidence the following:

> He called me fool.
> They took me prisoner.
> He was elected president.
> He was appointed ambassador.

In the first sentence one would normally expect

> He called me *a* fool.

In other words, the reference is usually to an instance, a person; this makes the article necessary. In the other three examples the nouns refer to a status, position or office, not to a person. The status of *prisoner*, or of *president*, or of *ambassador* is not normally to be considered numerical, hence the representation with a bare noun. *Fool* is not normally considered as a status, but as an instance, found *in* a particular person. One is not elected, appointed or taken fool; one is, or becomes, *a fool*.

We may in fact take this grammatical 'rule' and disprove it a thousand times by using attribute nouns that lend themselves to the representation of *instances* (*i.e.* numerical items), as opposed to a particular *status* or *position* (*i.e.* non-numerical items):

> This event made him a rich man.
> He was considered a failure.
> He called it an outrage.
> He really found me a nuisance.

It would even be possible, though the situational context would be rare, to add articles to the examples quoted above and produce:

[17] A. Bernier, *English Grammar* (Quebec, 1947), p. 40.

> They took me (a) prisoner.
> He was elected (a) president.
> He was appointed (an) ambassador.

provided that in each case the nouns *prisoner, president,* and *ambassador* were felt to be particular instances of the rank or status, and not the status or rank itself. The common usage with zero reflects the reality: rank and status are, for the most part, non-numerical. There is only one rank of *captain* in the army, no matter how many thousands of *captains* hold the rank; there is only one kind of wood called *oak,* but there are millions of *oaks* that provide the wood. The bare noun, calling into play as it does the great extensivity of notion belonging to the potential significate, presents the limitless, formless, continuate entity; when this vague representation must be limited, reduced, clarified, defined, refined, restricted, the article comes into play. *This is not dependent on 'rules', but on the representation sought by the speaker.*

The representation sought by the speaker will frequently be determined by the context. The same basic sentence shows different usages in different situations: a private in the army wishing to enjoy the status of commissioned rank would say:

> I want to be an officer.

This example is used by Zandvoort to illustrate the statement: "As a general rule it may be said that English uses the indefinite article before singular predicative nouns, and in adjuncts introduced by *as* and *for.*" This is another 'rule' that will not bear scrutiny. There are many different types of officer in the army, of all kinds of rank. There is no one rank of officer but many; the speaker can belong to only one rank (or instance of officer) at the one time. Hence the use of the article.

In another context, where the speaker belongs to an organisation that has a genuine *rank of officer,* the speaker might say

> I want to be officer.

just as an army man might say

> He's been captain for several years now.
> I expect he'll be major before very long.

E. ARTICLE WITH RANK, STATUS, PROFESSION

Now it is possible (and frequent) to find a noun of rank with the article:

> I want to be a lieutenant.
> He's been a captain for several years now.

These are instances, but instances of a type different from that found in

I want to be an officer.

Here *an officer* is an instance of *rank, a lieutenant* is an instance of *a rank.*

Instances of *rank* { Lieutenant 111111
Captain 11111111
Major 1111111111

Instances of
a rank

Figure V.1

See Figure V.1 for an illustration. Such contrasts are subtle and puzzling to a foreigner or indeed to anyone taking a general or precursory glance at the situation, but they are none the less real. Of these is woven the warp and the woof of everyday usage.

Perhaps this contrast can be seen more clearly in the case of a single office:

(i)   Dr. Arnold was headmaster of Rugby.
(ii).   Dr. Arnold was a headmaster of Rugby.

Example (i) gives a title of a man who lived at a certain period in history. No article is necessary since no one else could have held the office during the period that he held it — the view is synchronic; the expression *headmaster of Rugby* is a non-numerical singular. Example (ii) places Dr. Arnold in the long line of headmasters of Rugby, he becomes a mere instance, the expression *a headmaster of Rugby* is a numerical singular; the view is diachronic.[18]

Sometimes it makes little difference whether we suggest title or instance:

(i)   As coach he was a great success.
(i.e. in the role or status of coach)
(ii)   As a coach he was a great success.
(instance of profession)

The only difference between these two, either of which might be used in most situations, is that (i) emphasizes the job, the work done by the individual (qualitative), and (ii) emphasizes the person, the separate instance (quantitative). The force of such distinctions is often of little consequence.

There are of course many nouns applied to persons that rarely carry the sense of rank, status, profession, title, etc. This is especially true when these nouns are modified by an adjective, thus further reducing their chances of signifying total rank or status. Such a representation will always take the article:

He was considered a good student.
(Good student is not seen as a rank or status.)

Here again the stylistic overtones of quality and quantity may be observed.

The same is mostly true when those nouns that represent one office are modified by an adjective:

> Roosevelt was a hard-working president.
> *(Cf.* Roosevelt was president.)

This is not to be taken as totally true, however:

> As former coach he was not considered eligible.

This latter example could be used when there was only one former coach, a situation which restores the non-numerical view normally destroyed by an epithet, or else when the speaker wishes to bring out the qualitative aspect: "In his quality of former coach" Normally, however, one could expect an article.

F. ARTICLE WITH PERSONAL DESCRIPTION

English differs from other languages in some uses of the indefinite article. One is with nouns denoting parts of the body that are not continuate *(e.g.,* blood) or plural (teeth) in expressions of personal description:

> She has a small head.
> He has a pointed chin.

In this usage the Romance languages commonly use a definite article and place the adjective after the noun, the Germanic languages place the adjective before the noun and use an indefinite article.

Personal description poses the double problem of making clear the possessor and giving distinctive force to the description. The definite article is commonly used in the Romance languages to denote that the parts of the body so defined belong to the subject of the sentence. To solve the problem of personal description all that is needed is the addition of an attributive adjective, thus giving distinctive force to the description:

> Elle a la tête petite.

In the Germanic languages the attributive position of the adjective cannot be used since it carries with it the notion of a temporary, as opposed to a permanent, state of affairs:

> She has her hands black.

If the adjective is preposed, however, any anaphoric reference (definite article, possessive, *that*, etc.) will frequently run contrary to the sense desired:

> She has her small head.

This is not the presentation of a new fact of description, but reference to something we already knew; the description fails to be distinctive. The solution is to use an indefinite article:

> She has a small head.

In the plural or continuate there is no problem since zero article may have indefinite force:

> She has small hands.
> She has long hair.

In both singular and plural, however, there remains the possibility of an ambiguity,[19] showing that the solution to this problem of expression is really a makeshift.

G. ARTICLE WITH DISTRIBUTIVE SENSE

English uses the indefinite article in many cases where the noun has a distributive force, keeping the definite article to signify the unit of distribution:

> Butter is sold by the pound
> (The pound is the unit of measurement, but one may buy five pounds).

and the indefinite article for instances of the unit of distribution:

> Butter costs seventy cents a pound
> (*i.e.* each pound costs this).

H. SPECIAL STYLISTIC USAGE

There are also many cases where the system is exploited for purely stylistic purposes:

He had a conviction that the want of most men was knowledge of a sort which brings wisdom rather than affluence.[20]

It is possible in this passage to substitute definite articles and say *the conviction, the sort*, but this suggests (a) that the conviction is a common one (and therefore already known) and (b) that there is only one sort of knowledge which brings wisdom. The author suggests neither of these. In using the indefinite article he succeeds (1) in casting doubt on the validity of the conviction

---

[19] Are they *her* small hands?
[20] Example from Kruisinga, *Handbook*, Vol. II, p. 316.

(it was after all only one conviction among many possible) and (2) in suggesting that several sorts of knowledge bring wisdom, but any *one* will do.[21]

There is no end to the multiplicity and variety of usage that may be found.[22] Sometimes the use of the indefinite article is essential, sometimes one may obtain equally felicitous results with the definite article or the bare noun. We should not lose sight of the fact however that all usage, in all its complexity, is the reflection of a simple mechanical system to be found at the level of tongue. To attempt to explain usage without taking account of the system that lies behind it is to be lost in a wilderness of complexities; once the system has been correctly perceived, the usage can all be fitted into place.

I. CONCLUSION

The indefinite article occupies one half of the binary unit of the article system; it is the introductory movement toward the singular and particular. Placed in its normal syntactic position before the noun, it reduces the wide, vague notion of the bare noun to a singular instance. The definite article, as we shall see, takes over where the indefinite article leaves off.

---

[21] The indefinite article might also have been used with the noun *want* in the same quotation.

[22] Note, for example, the curious use of *a moon*: "A moon illuminated the island's flowerless garden" (Sillitoe, *Saturday Night and Sunday Morning*). *A moon* is a modification, appearance or phase of the moon. The usage shown here is impossible in French which must use an explicit modifier: *une lune pâle*.

VI

THE DEFINITE ARTICLE

A. DUAL ASPECTS OF THE DEFINITE ARTICLE

The definite article is the sign of an anaphoric withdrawal from the singular and particular towards the universal and general. Only a principle of movement can explain the two aspects of the definite article: its use to refer to things already mentioned and its use in making general statements of all kinds.[1]

The anaphoric usage of the definite article complements the introductory usage of the indefinite article. The indefinite introduces a specimen for the first time, the definite refers back to it. But the kinetic aspect of the definite article is always towards the universal and general, the kinetic aspect of the indefinite is always towards the singular and particular. As a result, the indefinite is frequently used for the presentation of *a particular instance*, the definite for a complete generality.

We have seen how the demonstrative *this* has an introductory force because it is the sign of an approach to the *hic et nunc* and how *that* has an anaphoric or referential force because it is a withdrawal from the *hic et nunc* already attained by the movement of *this*. This same contrast of introductory and referential force is to be seen in the system of the articles: the movement of approach to the singular and particular of which the indefinite article is the sign has an introductory force, the movement of withdrawal from this singular and particular, represented by the definite article, has a referential or anaphoric force.

Those peoples who speak the languages of the Indo-European family have a remarkable facility, not found to the same degree in other language communities and seemingly absent in some *(e.g.,* Chinese), of generalizing from a particular instance. It has often been remarked that Aristotelian logic is a purely Indo-European affair. Aristotle spoke of Induction, the main business of which is to lead on from the particular to the general, so that we see by a leap of intuition (Greek νοῦς) the laws of nature as exemplified in a particular instance. The physical sciences also aim at finding laws, and the theoretical and experimental methodology of these disciplines reflect Aristotelian induc-

---

[1] See above, pp. 69—70.

tion: the proposal of an axiom from a particular instance and the testing under experimental conditions to see whether this general statement may be considered true. The testing (Aristotle's "Complete Enumeration") is very necessary; without it the faculty or ability to generalize from a particular instance becomes dangerous and produces much shoddy and woolly thinking. But the important thing for us here is that this faculty is reflected in the usage of the general article. Before we can generalize inductively, we must present, or be presented with, the particular instance from which the further generalization is to be made. In the article system this task is done by the indefinite article. Once this has been performed we may, from the instance in mind, proceed to our generalization. This is the function of the definite article within the article system, hence its anaphoric value. It is used to represent items that we already *have in mind* through one cause or another.

B. THE ANAPHORIC ASPECT

If I start to talk about *a room*, I may immediately refer to it as *the room*. This is the most obvious anaphoric use of the definite article, but it is but a short step then to mention *the door, the floor, the ceiling, the windows, the walls, the furniture*. All these become anaphoric from the basic reference to *a room*. We may go even further than this; no particular notion need actually be introduced, but it may be present in the situational context and thus *in the mind*, in the consciousness or subconsciousness of the human being involved. It is in this way that the people who live in the same house may speak of *the garden, the back door, the garage;* the situation makes these cases as anaphoric as for the parts of the room above.

It follows that nothing could carry greater force of evidence in support of Guillaume's contention that language is man's means of representing and expressing a view of the experiential universe than the ordinary, everyday use of the definite article with the parts of the universe. People that live in the same house may talk of *the garden;* people that live in the same seaport may talk of *the harbour;* people that live in the same province may talk of *the province;* people that live in the same universe talk of *the universe, the sun, the moon, the stars, the sky, the heavens, the planets, the Milky Way, the Dog Star, the Big Dipper, the Earth and its parts, the North, the South, the East, the West, the Arctic, the Antarctic, the poles, the axis, the Equator* — the list goes on and on and all are anaphoric.

Anaphoric also are all the usages of the article with nouns relating to everyday human concerns and affairs: the parts of *the body: the head, the arms, the brain, the teeth, the lungs, the liver, the heart, the mind, the soul*. In similar fashion the anaphoric usage occurs with nouns that represent parts of our common understanding and background: *the past, the present, the future, the Norman conquest, the Armada, the Bible, the Queen, the Cold War.*

These anaphoric values may vary, following the range of values covered in the extensivity of the noun, from the particular to the generic. When we are talking of a particular sequence of events and proceed with the words *at the time,* this phrase refers to a very particular time already settled — the time of the particular sequence of events in question; the reference is, of course, anaphoric, without *a time* ever having been explicitly mentioned. Similarly we say *of the kind, from the evidence, for the record, by the way.* Nor do we require a prepositional phrase for this usage and value, provided we put our examples of *the kind, the evidence,* etc. in their right context so that they refer to a particular situation.

C. THE GENERIC ASPECT

We are familiar with the generic use of the definite article, the most common way of making generic statements about unit entities. Obviously it is more convenient to make a generic statement in an anaphoric reference than in an introductory statement, if for no other reason than that it is less convenient to generalize about that which is considered to be unfamiliar enough to need introduction than about that which is considered familiar and everyday. It follows that the indefinite, the article with the kinetic aspect toward the singular and particular, makes a less satisfactory generalization than the definite article whose kinetic aspect is always towards the general and universal.[2]

It is for this reason that the indefinite article is not always satisfactory for generic usage. Either article may be used in the sentence quoted by Christophersen as an example:

> The motor car is a practical means of conveyance
> A motor car is a practical means of conveyance

But when we change to *The motor car has become very popular,* we find that the indefinite article is no longer interchangeable. A single car is a practical means of conveyance, but a single car is not necessarily popular; what is popular is the total indivisible phenomenon of the motor car, and nothing less. The kinetic aspect of the indefinite article toward the singular and particular is an inhibiting factor which prevents the representation with the indefinite article from achieving the degree of generalization required.

---

[2] See above, p. 73. For a complete discussion of the question see Guillaume, "Particularisation et généralisation dans le système des articles français", *Français moderne,* Vol. XII (1944).

D. CONTRAST OF DEFINITE AND INDEFINITE WITH ZERO ARTICLE

The movement of the definite article begins at the singular and particular attained at the term of the indefinite article. From this *point de départ* already established, the movement continues with a more and more general representation until the limit of the article system is reached at a point where the representation is generic, but still unit: the entity represented is felt to have exterior form and therefore to be capable of multiplication to form a plural. It is not possible to multiply the formless — a thing must have form before it can be duplicated — and this contrast gives us in the English article system the threshold between the senses obtained on the one hand by the syntactic juxtaposition of the article (definite or indefinite) and by the bare noun (or article zero) on the other. To place an article alongside is to give form to the significate; without the article the significate remains vague, formless.

We have already seen that a noun like *letter* is normally used with an article:

> A letter is a means of communication.
> A letter arrived this morning.
> I opened the letter.
> The letter is a genuine literary form.

but that one can also produce a completely formless abstraction by the use of article zero:

> Letter was the one means of communication he had.

So it is that abstract nouns, normally continuate, expressing what is a continuum, in the generic use take no article:

> Beauty is Truth, Truth Beauty.

In similar fashion we talk of *generosity, goodness, stupidity, age, handiness, greed.*

E. GENERIC USE WITH SUBSTANTIVIZED ADJECTIVES

We may contrast the lack of article with abstract nouns with the use of the article with substantivized adjectives:

> Plato discussed the beautiful, the true, the good.
> *(Cf.* Greek: τὸ καλὸν, τὸ ἀληθές, τὸ ἀγαθόν)

The normal purpose of the abstract noun is the expression of quality: *beauty* is a quality. *The beautiful,* on the other hand, is not a quality, it is *the total sum of all that is beautiful,*[3] and normal usage is therefore quantitative, unit reference

---

[3] *Cf.* above, pp. 52—53.

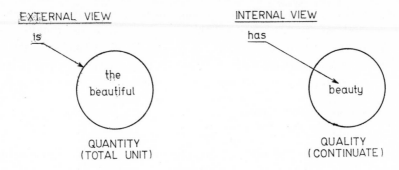

Figure VI.1

(see Figure VI.1). A philosopher might add that *beauty* is related to essence *the beautiful* to existence.

Because such constructions as *the beautiful* represent a discontinuum or sum of the total parts (exterior view) as opposed to the continuum expressed in the abstract noun (interior view), they do not share with continuate words the use of article zero, but use the definite article as do unit words. The bare adjective may not normally be used alone as a noun since the notion has no proper internal incidence.[4] The article limits the notion and gives it form — that of the totality of the objects where it is to be found — and thus supplies it with the necessary internal incidence. Under the actualizing force and influence of the article these words become capable of expressing, not just a *qualification*, but the totality of the objects so *qualified*.

Other remarkable things occur with these adjective-nouns. Since the notion is first of all adjectival before it becomes a noun, only the anaphoric use is possible and such words are never used in English with the indefinite article. Uses may be found, especially with adjectives of color that may also be full nouns in their own right, but always the force of a noun or pronoun is to be felt:

That yellow one is nice, but I think I'll have a blue (one).

People learning English as a foreign language are taught that they *must* put in the pronoun *one* in such a case as this, and a normal speaker of English would seldom or never indulge in the truncated form. In a similar situation a sentence such as *I've just bought a blue* turns out to be nonsense just because the reference to *one* is *completely* lacking. If we use *a blue* at all it is as the name (*i.e.*, as a noun) of a colour; as such it has a plural: *different blues*.

These substantivized adjectives are never used with indefinite reference because the aspect of the indefinite article is always toward the singular and

---

[4] An exceptional case with zero is dealt with, along with similar usage in the noun, in the chapter on article zero. See below, p. 127.

particular, whereas the aspect of the significate of the adjective, when the latter is used alone, is always toward the general because its significate, unlike that of the noun, lacks its own internal support. There is therefore a semantic clash of the indefinite article with the substantivized adjective just as there is with any other totally generalizing generic reference:

> *All a beauty of the world
> *(Cf.* All the beauty of the world)

There is a similar clash between plural reference and the indefinite article.[5]
Normally these adjectives used as nouns are singular:

> The good is to be sought by every man.
> The true is to be distinguished from the false.
> The beautiful was much discussed by Plato.

But when they are used to apply to a group of human beings, they take, without showing any morphological sign of the plural, a plural verb:[6]

> The blind are taught to read braille.
> The rich are the oppressors.
> The poor are the oppressed.
> The idle were forced to work.

The so-called proper adjective (written with a capital letter) also gives us the same construction:

> The English are a nation of shopkeepers.
> The Chinese were attacked by the Japanese.

These same adjective nouns may also be placed in apposition with a proper noun in the usage that is very common with numerals:[7]

> Charles the Second (written Charles II)
> February the fifth (February 5)
> Miss England the second (Miss England II — the name of a boat)

This usage is not limited to numerals, however:

> Charles the Bold
> Ethelred the Unready
> Jerusalem the golden
> Rome the eternal
> America the free

---

[5] And likewise between indefinite articles and nouns that resist the plural: *toast, machinery,* etc.
[6] See above, p. 53.
[7] See above, p. 57.

There is in some of these usages a flavor of poetic diction due to the unusual force of the substantivized, as opposed to the normal, adjective:

> In the streets of Babylon the old
> (Cf. the streets of old Babylon)

F. USE OF THE ARTICLE WITH PLURALS

Unlike the indefinite article the definite article may be used with plurals. It is noticeable, however, that the generic use in the plural takes no article, by way of contrast with the generic use in the singular:

> The telephone is useful to the businessman.
> Telephones are useful to businessmen.

At first view this seems somewhat surprising. The generic plural definitely represents a numerical notion, and it is also a total of the parts or discontinuum. We would expect such a usage to require an article. The answer to the problem lies in the -s that is the sign of the plural.

Where there is already a definer, an actualizer, the article is not used: no article is ever used with *this, that, these, those, my, your, some,* etc. Now the -s is also, in a different way, a definer, an actualizer; it realises the notion of plural and in so doing it attaches the numerical sense usually lent by the article in the singular. There can therefore never be a distinction between numerical and non-numerical in the plural; as a result the contrast between definite and zero articles is used in the plural to represent the contrast between anaphoric and generic. The normal generic plural does not need an article; so it is that in generic usage

> cripple*s* = *the* lame.

Here the -s of *cripples* is the sign of a discontinuum equal to that created by the article of *the lame*.

But the plural noun, by itself, without an article, is incapable of providing a finer representation of the plural than a plural of total or indefinite quality. When a definite, restricted plural is required, the article is called into play in order to provide the representation of definite quantity:

> Telephones are useful.
> The telephones in our office are always ringing.

In the second case the plural is strictly limited in extent as is shown by the prepositional phrase *in our office;* the reference is directly anaphoric.

G. EFFECT OF MODIFIERS ON THE USE OF THE ARTICLE

The grammarians have observed that a modifying adjective or adjective phrase juxtaposed to the noun may call into play the use of the article, and one might presume from this that an adjective *forces* the use of the article. This is not the case; again it is necessary to repeat that it is the representation sought by the speaker that causes the use of the article and rules cannot be deduced from the presence or absence of modifiers in the sentence.

From the point of view of representation it may be observed that the adjective has a different effect upon the noun significate if this latter is modified by the use of an article than if there is no article.

1. *Common nouns*

The effect of article zero on the singular common noun is to give an interior, qualitative view of the significate. As a result, the significate represents a formless, non-numerical continuate — there is no view of an exterior limit: *e.g.*, *oak*. The effect of the article, on the other hand, is to present an exterior, quantitative view of the significate; as a result a unit reference is obtained: *e.g.*, *the oak*.

These two views are essentially those of the *content* and of the *container*. When there is no article with the noun, the force of any modifier acts upon the qualitative view of the noun significate; when there is an article, the modifier affects the quantitative view of the significate:

Singular

> Fresh fish is hard to obtain (non-numerical, generic).
> The fresh fish we had yesterday was expensive (non-numerical, anaphoric).
> The fresh fish was a cod, the stale one was a halibut (numerical).

Plural

> Young horses are put out to graze (generic).
> The young horses are put out to graze (anaphoric).

It cannot be said that the use of adjectives or modifiers causes any difference of usage with the common noun.

2. *Proper nouns*

The proper noun, however, presents a different problem. The proper noun differs from the common noun in that the support of the potential significate is always an invariable. *The fish* may refer to any representative of the genus; a personal name on the other hand refers only to the individual concerned. As a result the qualitative and quantitative views of the significate of the proper noun do not normally differ — the content and the container are identical, and the article is unnecessary and therefore omitted; the qualitative view, because of the nature of the significate, by itself automatically suggests unit quantity.

When, however, a modifier is attached to a proper noun, the effect of modifying the quantitative, exterior view is quite different from that of modifying the interior qualitative view of the proper noun significate:

> The young Shakespeare would not have written that (quantitative, exterior view).
> Young Shakespeare would not have written that (qualitative, interior view).

It is notable that the phrase *the young Shakespeare* has a contrastive force that is lacking in *young Shakespeare:* there is an underlying contrast with *the older Shakespeare.* The reason for this is that the adjective affects the noun significate from its exterior, causing a limitation or *cut* in its total sense, thus providing a reduction of the total significate and the possibility of forming a contrast with the remainder. In the phrase *young Shakespeare*, on the other hand, the force of the adjective falls upon the interior view of the noun significate and is an *addition* to the totality of the significate. We may see this again with a modifying phrase:

> Peter down the street did that (continuate usage).
> The Peter down the street did that (unit usage).

In the first example there is not felt to be any differentiation from any other Peter, and the whole phrase is so semantically compact that it could be written *Peter-down-the-street.* The modifier has been added to the interior view of the significate to form a new total concept — the modifying phrase has become a part of the noun significate. The second example on the other hand suggests a contrast with another Peter, and the modifying phrase, acting upon the exterior view of the noun significate, exerts a restricting force.

Now it cannot be said that the adjective causes the use of the article in such instances. All that can be said is that when a modifier is attached to the significate of a proper noun there arises the possibility of a contrast between usage with definite and zero articles; a possibility that does not arise when there is no modifier. This possible contrast arises from the fact that either of the two possible views of the significate (container and content, which are identical if and when there is no modification) may be affected.

H. ARTICLE WITH PROPER NAMES OF PLACES

The question of adjectival force penetrates into the welter of usage to be found with the multitudinous types of proper names of places, some of which take articles, while others do not and some of which have adjectival parts in their formation:

> the Southern Cross
> Southern California

It will be my contention here that all such seeming adjectives, with rare and obvious exceptions, carry no distinctive force but are felt to be a part of the name. The common usage of English orthography, in writing such adjectives with a capital letter as if they were a part of the name, supports such a contention, but the real proof lies in the fact that usage of the definite article with proper names is not connected with the force of the adjective but on the nature of the thing represented and the speaker's view of it. *The Southern Cross*, for example, is a part of the firmament and fits into the category of a part of the universe as dealt with above (pp. 100—101); this is the anaphoric usage of the article. *Southern California* is the name of a state (California) which does not require an article; if a contrastive force were sought for the adjective, an article would be required; the adjective is therefore a part of the total name. The article is required with *Southern Cross* not because of a special force sought for in the adjective but because this name requires, like *the sun, the moon, the Plough, the Earth*, the anaphoric article used with the parts of the universe.

There are rare uses of adjectives that are felt to have real distinguishing force: when *Edgware Road* is thought of as *the road to Edgware* instead of as a mere name, then the name becomes *the Edgware Road*. Many of these differences disappear with time and the adjective becomes assimilated as a part of the total proper noun. This has happened, for example, with the eighteenth century names *the Green Park, the Regent's Park*, which today have become *Green Park* and *Regents Park*, even the possessive force having disappeared from the latter as shown by the common spelling. The same evolution may encompass such modern examples as *the Crystal Palace*, (made almost entirely of glass) and *the Royal Festival Hall* (built for the 1951 Festival of Britain) in accordance with *Buckingham Palace, Kensington Palace, Lambeth Palace*, and *Westminster Hall, Carnegie Hall*, although *the Albert Hall*, built as a memorial to Queen Victoria's husband, shows no sign of losing the article.

It is possible also, in the proper names of people (made up not of adjective and noun but of proper noun and common noun), for the preceding common noun to become a part of the total name and its distinctive force to be lost:

Colonel Johnson
Doctor Lawrence
Mister Boyd
Professor Crock
President Kennedy

But when the noun of rank, title, profession, etc. has not become a part of the proper name, it is felt as a common noun, to which the proper noun is juxtaposed in apposition, and which requires, therefore, an article:

The widow Osborne
The pilot Barecsz
The executioner Samson
The apostle Saint Paul
The Virgin Mary
The planet Mercury
The name Polonius[8]

Proper names of geographical places and objects can be divided according to whether (a) they require an article or (b) normally have no article. Of the compound names formed from a 'proper' adjective and what is normally a common noun (bay, ocean, etc.), we can make two distinct lists as follows:

Category (a): ocean, sea, river, canal, isthmus, peninsula, gulf
Category (b): street, avenue, square, road, place, crescent, bridge, mount, cape, lake, island, county, parish, point, bay, park

Examination of the types included in these categories shows that the objects represented in category (a) have for the most part an incomplete exterior boundary; it is impossible to say where the St. Lawrence River ends and the Gulf of St. Lawrence begins. The only doubtful one is *canal*. Most of the objects represented by nouns of category (b) have quite distinct external boundaries: lake, island, parish. The entities represented by *cape, mount, point* are themselves outlines or boundaries to the observer, and streets, roads, avenues and parks, etc., are felt to have defined, restricted boundaries that may be drawn on a map.

It may be objected to this classification that if a bay may be considered to have a clear exterior outline, then so may its counterpart, a peninsula. To this it can only be replied that the common experience of humanity (which can be expected to affect usage) is that one can see across a bay from point to point (an exact and obvious line) but that one cannot generally see across a peninsula. Furthermore one can draw on a map the line from point to point that limits a normal bay, but when one comes to draw a line that limits a peninsula, one can argue whether the line should be drawn at the narrowest point

---

[8]   Examples all from Kruisinga, *op. cit.*, Vol. II, p. 247.

in the neck (there might be two or more possible) or at some point where the apparent 'mainland' begins to widen into a larger land mass.

Whatever may be the final conclusion to such a discussion, this much is sure, that proper names representing a single entity of clearly defined outline resist the use of the article much more, and, from the historical point of view, much longer, than names that represent entities lacking definite, clear outlines. We have also seen that the purpose of the article is to lend form to what would otherwise be a formless representation; it creates a noun from an adjective by lending the form of the thing or things to which the adjective refers, by providing material content; it creates a unit noun out of a continuate by lending the form of the singular entity in which the continuate usually occurs: *oak* is found in *the oak*, *sun* (warmth, heat, sunlight) comes from *the sun*. Without the article the representation carried by the common noun lacks exterior form; the article provides exterior form.

For this reason proper nouns representing entities *(e.g.,* Lake Geneva, Vancouver Island) that have distinctive exterior form need no article in English since a bare noun may represent a real entity, and the representation, *because of the nature of the significate itself,* has adequate exterior form; the reference in this way presents a significate with clear exterior form without the intervention of the article being necessary.

Those proper names that represent entities where the limits or boundaries are incomplete or not clear and definite may take advantage of the clarifying power of the article. River names and the names of peoples, as we have seen, at first resisted the use of the article, but gradually developed the now regular article in the course of the evolution of the language. The names of single nations, states and provinces, felt in some languages to need the force of the article, have as yet not developed this usage in English.

There are on the other hand quite a few names of states or provinces that were not originally full proper names and therefore had a preceding article. Often the common noun element has disappeared, leaving a full proper name with an article that may continue or may in the course of time disappear. Compare the following:

> the Irish Free State
> the Transvaal (Republic)
> the Congo (Free State)
> the Labrador
> the Yukon
> the Klondike

The use of the article in *the Labrador* is due to the fact that for centuries the Labrador was merely a coast, it was not a territory with fixed boundaries — the basis of defining the boundaries of the Labrador was not laid down until the dispute before the Privy Council between Newfoundland and Canada was settled in 1927. The fishermen of Newfoundland have always gone *down on the Labrador coast* for the summer codfishery along the coast, and the expression became simply *down on the Labrador*.[9]

Today, with the boundary shown on the map and the development of the Labrador interior, the article is showing a tendency to disappear — no one says *in the Labrador*, the expression is always *in Labrador* and it is gradually replacing the older *on the Labrador*. Of a somewhat similar origin are *the Yukon* and *the Klondike*, both of them being in the beginning indeterminate areas around the channel of a river bearing the name.

I. ARTICLE WITH PROPER NAMES IN THE PLURAL

When there is a modifier with a singular proper noun, the article, as we have seen, may be used to obtain a contrasting force in the modifier. In referring to a lady I may call her *Miss Shaw*, but if there is a possibility of a confusion with another Miss Shaw, then I may say:

The Miss Shaw who lives in Town Row.

If the limiting adjunct does not need contrastive force, however, I may equally well say:

Miss Shaw who lives in Town Row.

But if I refer to two people of the same name and use a plural:

The Misses Shaw

the anaphoric article becomes necessary to prevent the reference from building into an unlimited plural:

(All) Misses Shaw.

A group of islands, limited in number, will thus require an article to prevent the suggestion of a common noun unlimited in number:

The Cyclades
The Bermudas *(Cf.* Bermuda)
The Philippines

---

[9] The reason for *down* in opposition to the common usage *up North* may be due to the fact that ancient navigation maps were drawn with the North at the bottom. A popular explanation from the fishermen is that the flood tide runs North and that one goes down with the flood tide.

And the same may be said of all plural proper names of places:

> The Netherlands
> The Americas
> The Indies
> The United States
> The Adirondacks
> The Himalayas

The article here is anaphoric and its purpose is to avoid ambiguity.

J. ARTICLE WITH NAMES LACKING COMMON NOUN COMPONENT

Another type of ambiguity also calls into play the use of the article with proper names. When a proper name normally containing a common noun component *(e.g.* Lizard *Point, Cape* Horn) drops this component from the name, thus losing an element of clarification, the article is frequently called into play to restore the lost clarification:

> to sight the Lizard
> to round the Horn

Proper names of common everyday objects tend in similar fashion to take an article if they have no common noun component:

> the Normandie *(Cf.* Normandy)
> the Queen Mary *(Cf.* Queen Mary)
> the Prado, the Vatican, the Louvre
> the Cumberland, the Ritz, the Savoy, the Queen Elizabeth (hotels)
> the Haymarket, the Odeon, the Palladium (theatres)
> the Mall, the Strand (but Whitehall, Piccadilly, Cheapside) (streets)
> the Thames, the Mersey (rivers)
> the Atlantic, the Pacific (oceans)
> the Jura, the Atlas (mountain ranges)
> the Bastille, the Kremlin, the Alcazar (fortresses)
> the Lyceum, the Athenaeum (clubs)
> the Solent, the Skagerrak, the Kattegat (bodes of water)

The foreign common noun is not considered as a common noun component:

> the rue de Provence *(Cf.* Oxford Street)
> the Place de la Concorde *(Cf.* Red Square)

K. PROPER NOUNS WITHOUT ARTICLE

The categories of such proper names that do not require the articles are (1) names of human beings and their pets, (2) place names of human geography, and (3) names of mountains. *e.g.:*

   (1)   Charles, Fido
   (2)   London, France, Scandinavia, Alberta, Ohio, Cornwall, Europe, Asia
   (3)   Everest, Snowdon, Kilimanjaro, etc. (but the Matterhorn, the Jungfrau, etc.)

A few minor exceptions to these basic categories may be found in some names, following local tradition and custom.

L. HONORIFIC ARTICLE

Of the more unusual uses of the definite article the typical and honorific article before both common and proper nouns has attracted much attention. It conveys a force equivalent to *the one and only* and may be seen in such instances as the following, displayed on a television screen as advertising for the station:

     Television is *THE* medium.

The following is also worth quoting (from Zandvoort, p. 118):

1. If any one in his ignorance were to ask, for instance, 'which river?', the answer might be '*the* river', *i.e.* the only, or the principal river in the neighbourhood; and the same with 'the Tower', 'the King', etc.

   Strong-stressed *the* can be used in a similar function before other class-nouns: she was *the* landlady *(i.e.* the typical landlady); it is *the* boot for present wear *(i.e.* the ideal boot).

It is interesting that this usage carries the same force of stress as the demonstratives *this, that,* etc. This value of the definite article lies just across the threshold from the indefinite article, *i.e.* at the beginning of the movement of the indefinite article; in Figure VI.2 it occupies position S_2.

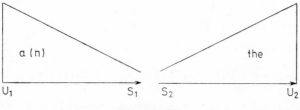

Figure VI.2

The value of this article differs only from that of the indefinite article at S_1 in that its reference is anaphoric, not introductory. It differs from the generic use of the definite article (U_2) in that it refers to a particular instance, not to all:

> Television is *THE* medium (of mediums)
> *(Cf.* the king of kings)

In comparing the use of definite and indefinite articles it can be seen how the definite article yields this particular value because of its anaphoric force:

> S_1 — Television is a medium (one of many)
> S_2 — Television is *THE* medium (the one of many, *i.e.* the one that stands out in value above the many)

Since there has been no prior mention of *a medium*, the anaphoric use carries the suggestion *the medium you should have in mind, the one you all know about, of course, the one you should be considering,* (because it is outstanding).

The usage of such an article was common among the Scottish clans to signify the chief. When everyone was called MacDonald, *the* MacDonald was the outstanding MacDonald, the head of the clan. This usage has never become very widespread in English.

Of a different origin is the use of this article with the names of prima donnas, actresses, and other temperamental females (and sometimes males), in imitation of the French and Italian usage:

> Last night the Siddons and the Kemble, at Drury Lane, acted to vacancy
> (qu. OED)
> the Dietrich and the Garbo (qu. Christophersen)

It is worth noting, however, that English more generally uses a demonstrative to translate this French and Italian article when used at the popular levels of speech:

> Où est-elle, la Louise?
> Where is that Louise?

The use of the article with the names of famous women may therefore be considered as a *calque* upon the French and Italian.

M. ARTICLE WITH COMPARATIVES

Perhaps the most unusual use of the definite article is as an adverb with the comparative of adverbs and adjectives:

> This appreciation of Agnes brought them into closer intimacy, and they talked the more easily of other things.
>
> Here, indeed, this freak of fortune was felt to be all the more cruel on account of the impossibility of resenting it.
>
> "But you know, Dr. Tempest, that you don't agree with your Bishop generally."
>
> "Then it is the more fortunate that I shall be able to agree with him on this occasion."[10]

There is no need to consider this *the* as another word because it comes from Old English *þe*, the instrumental case of the article. It little matters what it was in origin — the semiology of a language uses everything at hand, and there is no reason why an article should not function as an adverb if its force is found suitable in the particular adverbial construction.

It has just such a suitable force in these examples. An article is essentially a word used to limit or restrict the significate of the word that it syntactically precedes, and the definite article carries also an anaphoric force. Upon examination it will be found to limit the significate of the adverb or adjective that it modifies in these examples to a previously determined quantity — the latter is expressed by the definite article's referential force. In the first sentence *the* refers back to *closer intimacy*. We have seen that in talking about *the door, the windows, the kitchen* we are making an anaphoric reference to *the house;* a similar anaphoric reference is functioning here. The article also limits *more easily* to a quantity compatible with the *closer intimacy*. One could just as easily write:

> they talked *that much* more easily of other things.

This same anaphoric and limiting value can be seen in all the examples.

Of common currency in English is the use of the adverbial definite article in the correlative structure:

> The more the merrier
> The fewer the men the greater share of honour
> The more you do the more you may do

The function of the definite articles in these is to limit the two comparatives so that they equate. The condition/consequence force of the structure gives to the second *the* a greater anaphoric force than that to be found in the first, the main purpose of which is to suggest a range of quantity with fixed limits, but floating and free within those limits. Whatever restriction is imposed by the article in the condition is equalled in the consequence.[11]

---

[10]   Examples all from Kruisinga, *op. cit.*, Vol. II, p. 252.
[11]   The first *the* opens up an extensivity which is taken up by the second; the second is correlative to the first as *quam* is to *tam* in Latin *(tam . . . quam)*.

N. OMISSION OF ARTICLE WITH OTHER DEFINERS

In the presence of other definers the article, both indefinite and definite is suppressed. The following are never used with an article when they are attached to a noun:

> some, any, every, each, my, your, his, her, its, our, their, this, that, these, those, which, much

The possessive of nouns also causes the suppression of the article:

> George's book = the book of George

One must not make the mistake, in the possessive of common unit nouns, of attributing the article to the wrong noun. In *the barber's shop* the article belongs to *the barber* and not to *the shop*, the article of which is suppressed because of the possessive.[12]

O. CONCLUSION

The definite article occupies the second half of the binary system of the English article; its movement from the singular and particular to the universal and general is the inverse and the complement, the fulfilment, of the movement of the indefinite article. Both articles, being rooted in the singular and particular, bring to the noun, when preposed in their usual syntactic position, a force of restriction and limitation to either (i) a certain degree or (ii) to unit reference. For all that they impose a limiting force, there is a great range of extensivity within the confines of limited reference and unit reference, a range in fact from the particular to the generic.

Without the limiting force of the article, the noun expresses its total potential significate, limited only by the context of situation. When such a usage contrasts, *i.e.* yields a totally different sense from the usage with the article, then we may talk of an article zero, contrasting with, and complementing in the total system, the binary system of the indefinite and definite articles. It is to such an article that we now turn our attention.

---

[12] It is Zandvoort who inexplicably makes this error; see *Handbook*, p. 117.

VII

THE ZERO ARTICLE

A. SUBJECTIVE AND OBJECTIVE PRESENTATIONS WITH ZERO ARTICLE

In English the two articles are, among other things, signs representing two different ways of presenting a noun significate: an objective or introductory presentation (result of the movement of particularization) and a subjective or anaphoric presentation (result of the movement of generalization). It does not follow that a language that has no article system therefore lacks empirical distinctions between these two functions or lacks the possibility of making such distinctions. From the universally binary nature of article systems (even if the binary contrast is between definite and zero as in Classical Greek) we may deduce that it is something inherent in the system of the noun in the Indo-European languages that the binary system of the article reflects. We have proposed that the relationship of the particular and general senses of the potential significate are expressed at the level of tongue in a binary system; this binary system expresses movement (from U_1 to S_1 and from S_2 to U_2), the movement of the *acte de langage* or constructive processes of language, movement that is the activity of tongue, the final result of which will be the arrival of the significant at the threshold of the conscious mind. The thought of the speaker, having already a basic notion in view, scans the varying values of the potential significate and chooses that one, particularizing or generalizing, objective or subjective in presentation, which provides him with the representation he seeks. If there is no definer used and the language has an article system, the particular value of the representation will decide the use of the article: indefinite, definite or zero. If the language has no article system, the bare noun will be presented and the subjective presentations of the significate will often be indistinguishable from the objective ones. In a language that has no article system there is no distinguishing sign to mark the objective or subjective presentations.

It would be reasonable to ask on what grounds we might suppose the existence of these two types of representation in languages where there is no definite sign of their existence. It would be fatuous to suppose, in view of the changes and effects of linguistic form that the communication function of language has forged, that because the speaker is personally satisfied with the representation he be also satisfied with his inability fully to communicate his

representation to the hearer except by the manipulation of contextual opera-
tors. In concentrating on the speaker, too often ignored by theories of language
to their own detriment, we must not make the equal and opposite mistake of
ignoring the hearer.

The question can only be answered from hindsight, from observing the
growth of the article system itself. It is difficult to see what advantage may be
gained, when the noun is of such slight extensivity that it requires no article,
by identifying the subjective and objective presentations. All uses are so
much alike that no marker of any kind is concerned. The first change from this
system occurs when the extensivity of the *nom en puissance* widens and the
bare noun may be general, may be particular in reference. There now becomes
a need, for the sake of clarity, of marking the concrete anaphoric references,
and the definite article appears. For the time being, the introductory reference
is felt to be sufficiently general and vague to share article zero with the generic
reference; if a more particular introductory sense is required the numeral *one*
is used and it has a value of *a certain*.[1] When the extensivity of the *nom en
puissance* widens further, another need arises, that of distinguishing introductory references by means of their own marker; in English the numeral
becomes unaccentuated and neutralized in taking over this role, in other
languages the numeral retains the same form but it too develops into a separate
entity — the indefinite article.

From the viewpoint of a fully developed article system, having observed its
evolution, we can see that the genesis of the article follows this common pattern
because of the expression, implicit in the *nom en effet*, of the subjective and
objective perspectives which are to be found in the system of the *nom en
puissance*. It is, in other words, the binary contrasting of the values between
the singular and universal senses of the potential significate which yields these
two perspectives; and belonging to the *nom en puissance*, they are necessarily
reflected in the *nom en effet*. This reflection is to be perceived in the evolution
of article systems; it does not occur in other modifiers which are used either
uniquely with one perspective or indiscriminately with both.

We may now let our method itself carry us to a further development. There
is a binary contrast in English between continuate and unit usage in the noun.
Unit usage is expressed by means of an article, definite or indefinite, which
may be said to 'govern' the noun, using the noun for semantic content. The
article, definite or indefinite, in this way supplies an external, separate form
which is completed by the semantic content of the noun to produce numerical

---

[1] See above, pp. 72—74, for a more complete description and analysis of these developments.

or unit usage within the compact syntactic unit.[2] Continuate usage, on the other hand, uses the bare noun, without a syntactically separate form.

One may, therefore, in English, use a noun with or without a governing article. Without the article an interior view of the semantic content of the noun results; with an article it is an exterior view that is produced. This can be diagrammed by means of a now familiar figure (Figure VII. 1). There is,

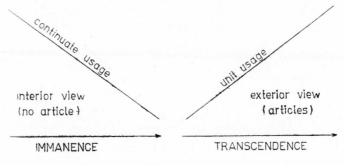

Figure VII.1

therefore, a double binarity in the article system, since the definite and indefinite articles form a separate binary system by themselves, a system that is based on the binarity of the subjective and objective presentations in the potential significate of the noun (Figure VII. 2).

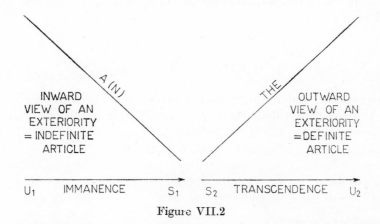

Figure VII.2

We must now examine continuate usage to see if there is a binarity of usage equal and complementary to the binarity of usage found in unit expression, since on purely methodological grounds we may expect to discover two types of zero usage to suit the theoretical binary structure (Figure VII.3). If these

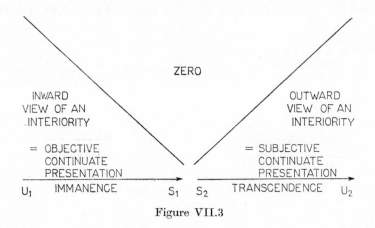

Figure VII.3

two values exist, we may expect the objective zero to differ from the subjective zero in the following regards: (a) the objective zero will express more easily the particular rather than the general because of its aspect toward the particular and singular, and (b) the subjective zero will more easily express the general rather than the particular because of its orientation toward the general and universal.

B. ZERO ARTICLE WITH SINGULARS

An examination of zero usage in English reveals that there are two main types of zero. Christophersen finds three that he calls *toto-generic, parti-generic* and *nulli-generic*, but this last is really the parti-generic or toto-generic usage after a negative. As examples he gives (pp. 33—34):

(1) The whole genus everywhere and at all times (toto-generic sense): lead is heavier than iron / time is money / history repeats itself.

(2) An indefinite amount of the genus (parti-generic sense): we are going to have tea soon / you are drawing water with a sieve / there is still frost in the ground / G. Eliot 538 I have caused sorrow already — I know — I feel it / Dickens PP 423 all seemed happiness and comfort / Seaford 52 She could say what she liked to Mr. Brook on paper / Strachey 107 with age, he seemed to acquire what was almost a new fervour / MGW 1935 the temperature of the air decreases with altitude.

(3) (In negative phrases) nothing of the genus (nulli-generic sense): I have not tasted food for three days / they never get rain in summer.

Of these three, Niels Haislund, in completing the final chapters of Otto Jespersen's *Modern English Grammar* (the great work left incomplete at his death), accepts the first two categories and says of the third:

But it may be doubted if it is necessary to set up a nulli-generic group. In the above two sentences I should say that the words *food* and *rain* are used in a parti- generic sense, representing in thought some positive quality, the existence of which then, it is true, is negatived by means of *not* and *never*. I am inclined to think that in most "nulli-generic" sentences we may rather speak of a parti-generic sense (rarely toto-generic).[3]

It is also worth observing that Christophersen himself does not insist very forcefully on the nulli-generic category. On page 34 he has a footnote on the three types:

It is practical, I think, in some cases to distinguish the first two types. The last one is of little importance and will as a rule not be exemplified in the following pages. — In French, on the other hand, the three types are kept formally apart: *J'aime le café / je bois du café / je n'ai pas de café.*

We have therefore two basic types of zero usage: the toto-generic and the parti-generic. Of these two the parti-generic usage is zero presentation of the objective, the toto-generic is the zero presentation of the subjective.

There are not, however, two distinctive zero forms, and it becomes appropriate therefore to treat zero as a single article, standing in contrast to the combined indefinite and definite articles; the result is another common linguistic mechanism, a double binary or ternary system:

zero	indefinite	definite
interiority of an interiority	interiority of an exteriority	exteriority of an exteriority
IMMANENCE	TRANSCENDENCE[1]	TRANSCENDENCE[2]

(For another double binary system, see page 51. Compare also the system of grammatical person: first, second and third; or the system of positive, comparative and superlative in the adjective).

---

[3]   *Modern English Grammar*, Vol. VII, p. 441.

C. ZERO ARTICLE WITH PLURALS

It is interesting to see how the plural usage exactly parallels the continuate usage of the singular. We can discern two zero plurals, a parti-generic and a toto-generic.[4] Christophersen gives the following examples:

(1) Toto-generic sense: Isaac Watts (qu. Bartlett 150) Let dogs delight to bark and bite, for God hath made them so — thoughts are sometimes difficult to put into words / Shakespeare Tp. IV. i. 156—7. We are such stuff / As dreams are made on.

(2) Parti-generic sense: Delafield 21. They ate ices and wandered about / to make purchases / G. Eliot 538 I could commit crimes for you / ib. 551 We judge others according to results / A. H. Thompson 774 She was a victim to ill-health, which grew upon her with years (compare the equivalent phrase "with age").

The toto-generic plural is a subjective zero, the parti-generic plural is an objective zero. Both are generic, but the aspect of the former is toward the general, the aspect of the latter toward the particular. Both objective and subjective presentations, in other words, may receive the sign of the plural.

In the plural there is no contrast of numerical and non-numerical since any plural, by definition, is numerical. There is therefore no continuate representation in the plural, only unit reference: the plural represents the sum of n units. Furthermore the plural morphology already represents this unit reference satisfactorily, so that there is no need for the article to act as a sign of the numerical, as in the singular.

As a result, the plural resists the use of the indefinite article and normally restricts usage of the definite article to anaphoric reference.[5] The indefinite article may, however, be used with singular collectives: *a few, a dozen, a hundred;* and these singular collectives, because of their plural content (lexical internal plural) may be used, like other numerals, with plural nouns: *a few men, a dozen eggs.*[6]

Possible plurals are therefore as follows:

Objective zero:	*tables*
Subjective zero:	*tables*
Objective with article:	*(a few tables)*
Subjective with article:	*the tables*

---

[4]   Plurals also resemble singular continuates in usage in that they may be modified by *some, any* and *all,* but resist *every* because of its uncompromisingly singular reference.

[5]   Article usage with plurals in Modern English is quite similar, therefore, to the usage with singulars in Old English; this is due to the lack of continuate reference in the plural.

[6]   In these cases the modifier has a plural content. In other cases, by contrast, the combination numeral + noun may be considered as a singular unit: *a long five miles, a big twenty-four inches high.*

The question immediately arises as to how the two types of zero plural are to be distinguished in discourse since they bear no distinguishing morphological marks.

First let it be said that the context frequently decides for both speaker and listener, as in our examples above. Christophersen also comments:

A universalized phrase encroaching upon the domain of a parti-generic one is hard to recognize. As the two are alike in form, it may not be possible in a given case to tell which of the two was intended by the author (who probably did not realize the difference himself). The universalized form contains an element of familiarity which is absent in the normal form, but in many cases it makes no difference whether the phrase is understood in one way or another.

Often modifiers may be used to show clearly whether an objective or subjective plural is intended. Ordinary numerals, for example, normally mark a subjective plural, but the objectifying force of *some* when added to the reference may show an intention to express an objective value:

> Some fifteen men were present.

This produces a reference similar in force to *a dozen men*, which is quite obviously objective because of the use of the indefinite article.[7]

Although the existence of objective and subjective presentations in the plural can be demonstrated, they do not have any remarkable notional contrast and therefore do not have a distinguishing morphology. It is appropriate therefore to follow the policy established for the singular and to treat zero as a single article.

D. USE OF ZERO ARTICLE TO PROVIDE CONTINUATE AND AVOID UNIT REFERENCE

English makes frequent use of the zero usage not only to avoid the image of the singular to be found in unit usage, but often merely to avoid the connotations inherent in the unit representation. Christophersen, confused by the conflicting usage even goes so far as to suggest "misuse" of zero usage (p. 108): "In recent times a tendency has sprung up to use (one might almost say 'misuse') the zero-form even where the *the*-form would seem to be required." This tendency is shown in what might be called 'quasi-personification'. When we say:

> Rumour has it that ...
> Legend relates that ...

---

[7]   In French such numerals are expressed in a singular collective with the singular aspect: *une quinzaine, une vingtaine*. This is one solution to the clash of plural notion with singular content.

one might just as easily use an article, either definite or indefinite. The difference is that here zero article is chosen to give the noun a continuate sense — the representation of rumour and legend as they function in the experience of mankind, and not a particular rumour or a particular legend. This is common with nouns such as the following:

> interest, tension, conversation, life, tradition, unemployment, co-operation, disillusion, publication, contact, acquaintance, ignorance, folly, stupidity, cleverness, experience, contrast, release, escape, work, traffic.

Modifiers, whether adjectival or phrasal, do not affect the use of the article:[8]

> Popular interest in Shakespearian comedy
> Public interest in international affairs
> Tension in France over the incident
> Life at sea is somewhat monotonous
> Publication of the letters followed
> Ancient tradition was upheld
> Early release of the prisoners was expected

Christophersen claims that material words (or, as he calls them, "pure names of substances", such as milk, air, iron, butter, etc.), are immune against the influence of this tendency. The following gleaned from the daily newspaper contradict the assertion and represent what will be recognized as a common usage:

> *Steel* for the new building arrived some time ago.
> They estimated that *furniture* damaged by the fire was worth more than $100,000.

The purpose of all these instances of zero is the avoidance, for one reason or another, of exact or unit reference, and the providing of a representation lacking in clear outline and limit. *Popular interest* and *public interest* are unknown quantities, as are *Tension in France*, *Steel for the new building*, and *furniture damaged by the fire;* as a result anaphoric or unit reference is avoided. The vague reference informs us that the quantity in each case is unknown or uncertain to the speaker. With these references we can add the modification *Whatever . . . there was* and the same effect is produced. *Life at sea* is all life at sea, an unlimited generic, and the normal expected usage here; *Ancient tradition* is also an unlimited generic, and the sentence suggests that not only was the particular tradition upheld but that all ancient tradition was upheld; as a result the reference has a somewhat more dramatic flair than the usage with an article. *Publication* and *Early release* are actions, and continuate representation is sought in order to present the action in progress, in its imperfective aspect,

---

[8]   See above, pp. 106—107.

whereas the use of an article would lend a sense of completeness (unit usage !) to the noun, showing the action involved under its perfective aspect.

Many different results are produced by the contrast of unit and continuate usage. We have a natural sense of the finite limitations of tongue and therefore refer always to *the English Language;* the usage without the article represents something quite different — studies or instruction in the language, which are not finite, but continuate:

> He obtained high marks in *English Language.*

Football is a game, *the football* is the ball with which it is played; *thought* is *la pensée pensante*, *the thought* is *la pensée pensée* (note the correspondence with *(the) publication, (the) release:* imperfective/perfective); *night* is darkness, *the night* is the time of darkness.

We enjoy *sun* or *shade* in the summer, but we sit in *the sun* or *the shade* (the place where there is sun or shade). We drink *water* (continuate) from the tap but swim in *the water* (the place where there is water). We breathe *air*, but throw a ball in *the air;* horses eat *grass*, but lie down on *the grass;* we buy *land* but live on *the land*. Similarly we speak *German* but translate a work from *the German* (found in the particular book).

E. ZERO ARTICLE WITH THE NOUNS *MAN* AND *WOMAN*

Man is mankind, both masculine and feminine, or restrictively masculine; it represents the human race conceived non-numerically, in continuate fashion.[9] *Woman* similarly means womankind, again continuate. These continuates are to be distinguished from the continuates *oak, horse, chicken*, etc., which represent material content (in this case wood and meat); *man* and *woman* emphasise the non-material content common to all humans, namely the continuate that is human consciousness. Each man sees himself mirrored in the continuate of his own consciousness, and knows his fellows in like kind. The material expression is to be found in the plural *men*. *The man* is reserved for the separate individual male as in Wordsworth's often quoted

> The child is father to the man.

The child is not the father to *man* (the continuate), but only to the separate individual that each child grows into.

The grammars of English usually state that 'class nouns' in the generic sense require an article, with the exception of *man* and *woman*, and quote examples such as the following:

---

[9] See also above, p. 24, and the quotation there from *The Screwtape Letters.*

The dog, the house, the city, the state, the book.
The horse is useful to *the farmer*.
The horse is useful to *man*.

The individual human being does not belong to the categories of *dog, house, etc.*, but he does belong to the category of *man*. We should not be surprised, therefore, that in this instance the interior, qualitative view of the significate is preferred over the exterior, quantitative view. The article with *woman* is omitted for the same reason, although it is used more often than with *man:*

Man is for the woman made.

This example is taken from an old song which was remade in recent years into a popular song.

F. ZERO IN OTHER CONTINUATE SENSES

It is in a somewhat similar fashion that *school, prison, church,* etc, represent the continuate non-material aspect of the material units *the school, the prison, the church,* etc. The child goes to *school,* the parent goes to *the school* to see the child's teacher. One may go to *school* at home or go to *church* in *the school;* one can in fact go to *school* or *church* without going near *the school* or *the church.*

It is this usage that is also the origin of *keep house, teach school.* When the object of the verb is not restricted to a particular, no article is used. Lists of these expressions are to be found in the grammars. Here are a few examples:

take office
declare war
weigh anchor
break surface
keep faith
take offence
give way
make room
abandon ship
play ball
give chase
bear malice

Very often with such expressions the two words come into such consistent close contact that they may be felt as a unit. This is a common enough phenomenon in other languages: *Cf.* French *faire feu, perdre patience.*

Zero usage after prepositions reflects normal zero usage. *A car* is a unit item, *car* is a means of transport, a continuate. Means of transport and communication are often presented in a prepositional phrase:

by letter
by radio
by word of mouth
by steamer
by bus
on foot
on horseback

Zero after prepositions is therefore continuate usage as found in other syntactic situations.

G. ZERO IN ENUMERATIONS AND PAIRS OF WORDS

Often when two closely related words stand together, the article is omitted before the second:

the king and queen
the father and mother
the brother and sister

In such a case the defined first noun may be said to give unit representation to the second which follows directly and is closely related in sense.

This use of one noun to define another may be used to work in both directions at once, so that two or more nouns in usages that normally require an article have zero. This occurs when natural pairs, groups and ranges are expressed together:

day after day
from head to toe
bag and baggage
body and soul
diamond cut diamond
dog eat dog
mouth to mouth
from father to son
lock, stock and barrel
hunter and hunted
land and sea
man to man
untouched by painter, carpenter or bricklayer
They came with banner, spear and shield

And even the following are to be found in very common everyday currency:

high and low, rich and poor

This usage is to be found in all syntactic positions (all examples quoted in Jespersen, *Modern English Grammar*, Vol. 7, pp. 464—8):

(1) Subject
Brother and sister were at breakfast
(2) Object
Kitty hurriedly gathered up gloves and fan
(3) Subject and object together
dog succeeded dog, and apartment succeeded apartment
(4) After preposition
twirling the stem of a wine-glass between thumb and first finger
(5) With two prepositions
it has to grow, and to be handed down from father to son
(6) Predicate of 'to be'
I can't be buyer and seller too

It is also found regardless of whether the sense is continuate or unit, generic or particular:

(1) Generic unit
For oak and elm have pleasant leaves
(2) Particular unit
Chaucer's range from knight to miller, from aristocratic prioress to bourgeois wife of Bath
(3) Generic continuate
To sea and wind and flame
(4) Particular continuate
She had lost *youth, fortune,* child and husband

It is remarkable that these zero nouns must belong to the same immediate syntactic structure, otherwise the article will be used:

'Tis funny how *rogue knows rogue*

But:

Set a thief/to catch a thief

Belonging in this fashion to the same syntactic structure, each noun reacts upon the other in a way that makes the article unnecessary; as a result the article disappears with astonishing frequency, it does not stay where its presence is not needed in spite of Gardiner's assertion that "Often it is mere useless ballast, a habit or mannerism."

The zero nouns in this usage must not only be in the same syntactic structure, they must also be known as, or felt to be, a part of each other, or of a larger whole, group, team or range. It is in this way that they limit each other; if they are even remotely unrelated the article must be used:

I settled myself in my chair and, *putting match to gasper,* awaited the inside story.

But:

> I put *a match* to *his cigarette.*

It is also remarkable that the plural, although found in this usage, is rare and the singular dominates:

> from head to foot
> from tip to toe
> horse and foot, cannon and tumbrel, drum and standard
> three men came marching along, pipe in mouth and sword in hand[10]

This would suggest that the limiting force applied by one noun upon the other in the group is not as great as the force applied by the article, and a lesser degree of actualization is produced, which is, however, suitable for the particular context where such zero usage is found. The stylistic effect is frequently one of intimacy — the listener or reader is presumed to be familiar enough with the rest of the situation for the items to be clearly actualized; the interior view of the significate is sufficiently limited in such a situation to convey a similar sense to that of the external view.

H. INTIMATE USE OF ZERO

The zero usage for familiar household personalities helps to clarify this statement:

> Father is angry
> Cook has given notice
> Nurse is out

These are all part of a group or team who are known so intimately to one another that the article may be dispensed with among them even when no other part of the group is mentioned in the same syntactic structure.

Such familiarity may be seen also in the usage with the name of a governing body of a country. Genuinely foreign governing bodies always have an article:

> The Bundestag, the Diet, the Duma

But the governing body of a particular people may be named by them (and their neighbours) without an article:

> Congress is in session
> Parliament opens to-morrow

---

[10] Cf. *our hearts leaped to our mouths.* Example qu. Jespersen, *Philosophy of Grammar,* p. 191.

The same is found in the somewhat archaic expression:

Holy Mother Church

Such usage has almost the same status as a proper noun.

I. CONCLUSION

All zero usage has, in fact, similar status to the proper noun; a zero noun calls into play a total significate (even if viewed from a particular aspect) exactly as does the proper noun. We may therefore equate the following usages:

John is dark.
Man is mortal.
Butter is yellow.
Generosity is laudable.

Reduction or other modification of this total significate calls into play in most contexts the use of the article or of other definers. In those contexts where zero usage persists even with a significate modified from the possible total whole, familiarity produced in the total situational context (by either words or knowledge) forms a sufficient alternative actualizing force and thus permits a zero usage.

VIII

CONCLUSION

The immediate study of this essay has been the functioning of the article system of English and its relationship to the noun. Implicit in the approach, however, is a more profound study — the examination of the nature of language in all its aspects.

The article system of English provides a good basis for such a study for several reasons: (1) Its historical evolution can be observed from both the structural and the phonetic points of view; (2) This historical evolution can be compared with that found in other, different languages; (3) The structural system of the article is not directly observable and the researcher is therefore forced into an analysis of the substructures of language that can only be said to exist in the subconscious levels of the mind *(i.e.,* in tongue); (4) The definite and indefinite articles are among the ten most frequent words of English discourse, their usage and stylistic manipulation affect a tremendous range of discourse; and (5) The nature of the article system in English throws light on the type of language that is found in the Indo-European family of languages.

In Chapter I the obvious facts concerning the historical development of the article system in English are presented, and comparisons made with article systems in other languages of the Indo-European family. The relationship of the rise of article systems to the disappearance of the eight case system of the Indo-European noun is discussed in terms of the dematerialization of the significate of the *nom en puissance.*

Since the work of Guillaume is but little known, it was necessary in Chapter II to give an outline of some of his ideas and to attempt to place them in the background of modern linguistic thought. The sketch is necessarily inadequate, since a thorough undertaking of such a project would take a separate volume.

Chapter III treats the question of the noun in English from a theoretical viewpoint, relying heavily for explanation and clarification on Guillaume's ideas of binarity, incidence, plurality, dematerialization and linguistic evolution. Chapter IV states the 'classical' Guillaumian view of the functioning of an article system, applied to English, and gives a glimpse of the results obtainable with psychomechanical analysis by demonstrating, for the sake of an analogical example, the functioning of English demonstratives.

The final three chapters are devoted to the explanation and clarification of usage when seen from the point of view of the psychomechanical system of the articles. Chapter V examines usage found with the indefinite article, Chapter VI that found with the definite article, and the final chapter investigates the usage and semantic force of the bare unqualified noun, or to use the common terminology, of the zero article.

It is certain that not everything has been said in this essay that could be said about the articles: usage, for example, is infinite, and no attempt has been made, nor, in all conscience, could be made, to explain it exhaustively in all its aspects. What has been done is the presentation of a system which the reader himself can utilize, if it makes sense, to explain or classify usage that he may encounter.

It has been assumed in this study that linguistic structure functions along patterns that are mechanical, and is to be explained in mechanical, not logical terms. Even Jespersen, for all his insights into the functioning of language, on occasion overlooks this fundamental point:

In cases like the *English* king / the king *of England* / the *eldest* boy / the boy *who stole the apples*, etc. the adjuncts here printed in italics are in themselves quite sufficient to individualise, and the article may be said so far to be logically superfluous though required by usage, not only in English but in other languages.[1]

We can see here, to take only one example, that *king of England* (without the article) means the position or title (continuate, non-numerical view), whereas *the king of England* makes reference to the person. This eludes Jespersen because he has not taken into account the mechanical nature of the article system.

The system of the articles is, furthermore, a mechanism, or better a psychomechanism, that is of some importance in tongue. On page 25 of *Le Problème de l'article* Guillaume comments:

L'article est quelque chose qui 'emploie' le nom. Cela lui donne *une place spéciale parmi les êtres du langage,* et le range au nombre des éléments qui peuvent, à un moment donné de leur progrès, — lorsqu'ils se sont systématisés suffisamment, — relever d'une étude raisonnée. Car si le langage en lui-même n'est pas 'intelligent', du moins le fait de l'employer est-il un 'fait intelligent'. Ceci est hors de doute. Il s'ensuit que si quelque chose dans le langage emploie le langage, ce 'quelque chose' se trouve agir dans le même sens que la pensée, dont il reproduit les mouvements.

This comment, now half a century old, reveals an aspect of the phenomenon of language that Guillaume was to examine and develop further over the years in analysing the relationship of language and thought. His view was always

---

[1]   Jespersen, *Philosophy of Grammar*, p. 109.

that the patterns of thought and the patterns of language are inexplicably and ineluctably interwoven — are, in fact one and the same. Any light shed on one automatically yields insight into the other.

There remains, then, the great and difficult task of relating the mechanism of the article system to that of other similar linguistic systems through an investigation of the whole means of representation utilized by speakers of English. From such an investigation we may gain profound insight upon our modes of thought and perception, but the ultimate goal will be, for the linguist, the perspectives that these latter, once revealed, can open upon the means of representation and expression of human language. Nor is this final aim merely esoteric; we should not lose sight of the fact that language is the core of all our knowledge, since through its intermedium we largely perceive, reflect upon and remember, through every fleeting moment of our conscious existence, the universe in which we live.

BIBLIOGRAPHY

Ahlgren, A., *On the Use of the Definite article with 'Nouns of Possession' in English*,
  Stockholm Studies in English II (Stockholm and Uppsala 1946); also Stockholm
  diss. (1946).

Barnet, L., *The Universe and Dr. Einstein*, 2nd. rev. ed. (New York: Mentor Books, 1957).

Bernier, A., *An English Grammar* (Québec: Semaine commerciale, 1947).

Bloomfield, L., *Language* (New York: Holt, 1933).

Bonfante, G. U., "Semantics in Linguistics" in *Encyclopaedia Britannica* (1958 ed.),
  Vol. 20, pp. 313D—313H.

Brain, Sir Russell, "The Semantic Aspect of Aphasia" in *Archivum Linguisticum* 8, 1:
  20—27, (1956).

Brunner, Karl, *Outline of Middle English Grammar* (Oxford, 1963).

Chomsky, N., *Aspects of the Theory of Syntax* (MIT Press, 1965).

—, *Current Issues in Linguistic Theory* (The Hague: Mouton, 1966).

—, *Language and Mind* (New York: Harcourt Brace, 1968).

—, *Syntactic Structures* (The Hague: Mouton, 1957).

Christophersen, P., *The Articles: a Study of their Theory and Use in English* (Copenhagen
  and London, 1939); also Copenhagen diss. (1939).

Delbrück, B., "Das schwache Adjectivum und der Artikel im Germanischen" in *Indogermanische Forschungen XXVI* (Berlin, 1909), pp. 187—199.

Elcock, W. D., *The Romance Languages* (London: Faber, 1960).

Firth, J. R., *Papers in Linguistics 1934—1951* (London: OUP, 1957).

Funke, O., "On the Attributive Adjective in OE Prose and Early ME" in *English Studies*,
  XXX (1949), 151—6.

Gallup, J., "An Approach to the Theory of Declension" in *Canadian Journal of Linguistics*,
  Vol. 8, No. 1 (1962), pp. 26—32.

Gardiner, A. H., *The Theory of Speech and Language* (Oxford: Clarendon, 1932).

Guillaume, G., *L'Architectonique du temps dans les langues classiques* (Copenhagen:
  Munksgaard, 1945).

—, *La Langue est-elle ou n'est-elle pas un système?* Cahiers de linguistique structurale
  (Québec: Presses Universitaires Laval, 1952).

—, *Langage et Science du langage* (Quebec and Paris, 1964).

—, *Temps et Verbe* (Paris: Champion, 1929).

—, "Logique constructive du système des articles" in *Français moderne*, XIII (1945),
  pp. 207—229.

—, "Particularisation et généralisation de l'article" in *Français moderne*, XII (1944),
  pp. 89—107.

—, *Le Problème de l'article et sa solution dans la langue française* (Paris: Hachette,
  1919).

—, "La Question de l'article" in *Français moderne*, XIII (1945), pp. 70—82.

Henry, V., *Grammaire comparée de l'allemand et de l'anglais* (Paris: Hachette, 1906).

Heinrichs, H. M., *Studien zum bestimmten Artikel in den germanischen Sprachen* (Giessen:
  Wilhelm Schmitz, 1954).

Hill, A. A., *An Introduction to Linguistic Structures* (New York: Harcourt Brace, 1958).

Hodler, W., *Grundzüge einer Germanischer Artikellehre* (Heidelberg: Carl Winter, 1954).

Jespersen, O., *The Philosophy of Grammar* (London: Allen and Unwin, 1924).

—, *Growth and Structure of the English Language*, 9th ed. (Oxford: Blackwell, 1958).

—, *A Modern English Grammar*, Part VII, completed and published by Niels Haislund (Copenhagen: Munksgaard, 1949).

Katz, J. J., "Mentalism in Linguistics" in *Language* 40: 124—137.

Kneale, W. C., *Probability and Induction* (Oxford nd New York: Clarendon, 1949).

Kruisinga, E., *A Handbook of Present Day English* (Groningen: Noordhof, 1932).

Lees, R. B., *The Grammar of English Nominalizations* (The Hague: Mouton, 1960).

McClean, R. J., "The Use of Ein with Plurals in German" in *Modern Language Review*, XLVIII (1953), pp. 33—38.

Meillet, A., *Caractères générales des langues germaniques*, 4th ed. (Paris: Hachette, 1930).

—, *Introduction à l'étude comparative des langues indoeuropéennes*, 8th ed. (Paris: Hachette, 1937).

Mittins, W. H., *A Grammar of Modern English* (London, 1962).

Mustanoja, T. F., *A Middle English Syntax*, Part I (Helsinki: Société Néophilologique, 1960).

Ogden, C. K. and I. A. Richards, *The Meaning of Meaning*, 4th ed. (London: Routledge, 1936).

Penfield, W. and L. Roberts, *Speech and Brain Mechanism* (Princeton: University Press, 1959).

Prokosch, E., *A Comparative Germanic Grammar* (Baltimore: Linguistic Society of America 1938).

Robbins, Beverly L., *The Definite Article in English Transformations* (The Hague: Mouton, 1968).

Robins, R. H., *General Linguistics, An Introductory Survey* (Longmans, 1964).

Sapir, E., *Language* (New York: Harcourt Brace, 1921).

—, *Selected Writings* (California University Press, 1949).

de Saussure, F., *Cours de linguistique générale*, 3rd ed. (Paris: Payot, 1955).

Sauvageot, A., *L'Emploi de l'article en gotique* (Paris: Champion, 1929).

Stern, G., *Meaning and Changes of Meaning* (Göteburg, 1931).

Streitberg, W., *Gotisches Elementarbuch* (Heidelberg: Carl Winter, 1920).

Sweet, H., *Anglo-Saxon Primer*, 9th ed., ed. Davis (Oxford: University Press, 1953).

Süsskand, P., *Geschichte des unbestimmten Artikels im Alt- und Frühmittelenglischen*, SEP LXXXV (Halle, 1935).

Twaddell, W. F., *On Defining the Phoneme*, Language Monograph No. 16 (Linguistic Society of America, 1935).

Ullmann, S., *The Principles of Semantics*, 2nd. ed. (Oxford: Blackwell, 1957).

Valin, R., *Petite Introduction à la psychomécanique du langage* (Québec: Presses Universitaires Laval, 1953).

—, *La Méthode comparative en linguistique historique et en psychomécanique du langage* (Québec, 1964).

—, "Grammaire et logique: du nouveau sur l'article" in *Travaux de linguistique et de littérature*, V, 1: 61—74 (1967).

—, "Qu'est-ce qu'un fait linguistique?" in *Français moderne*, Vol. XXVII, pp. 85—93.

Vater, H., *Das System der Artikelform in gegenwärtigen Deutsch* (Tübingen, 1963).

Wiener, Norbert, *Cybernetics*, 2n ded. (MIT Press, 1961).

Zandvoort, R. W., *A Handbook of English Grammar* (London: Longmans, 1957).

INDEX

JANUA LINGUARUM

STUDIA MEMORIAE NICOLAI VAN WIJK DEDICATA

Edited by. C. H. van Schooneveld

SERIES PRACTICA

52. RUTH MARGARET BREND. A Tagmemic Analysis of Mexican Spanish Clauses. 1968. 128. pp. Gld. 33.—
53. HAROLD H. KEY: Morphology of Cayuvava. 1967. 73 pp. Gld. 22.—
55. L. ROMEO: The Economy of Diphthongization in Early Romance. 1968. 127 pp. Gld. 30.—
57. ALAN CAMPBELL WARES: A Comparative Study of Yuman Consonantism. 1968. 100 pp Gld. 30.—
58. JEAN PRANINSKAS: Trade Name Creation: Processes and Patterns. 1968. 115 pp Gld. 30.—
59. GEORGE GIACUMAKIS JR.: The Akkadian of Alalah. 1970. 119 pp. Gld. 36.—
60. JOAN RUBIN: National Bilingualism in Paraguay. 1968. 135 pp. Gld. 40.—
61. SALMAN H. AL-ANI: Arabic Phonology: An Acoustical and Physiological Investigation. 1970. 104 pp.
    18 figs. 16 examples, 13 illustr., 3 diagrams. Gld. 36.—
62. CURTIS P. HEROLD: The Morphology of King Alfred's Translation of the Orosius. 1968. 80 pp. Gld. 24.—
63. JAN SVARTVIK: On Voice in the English Verb. 1966. XIV + 200 pp., figs. and tables. Gld. 32.—
64. MARVIN R. WILSON: Coptic Future Tenses: Syntactical Studies in Sahidic. 1970. 143 pp.
    Gld. 40.—
65. RUSSEL N. CAMPBELL. Noun Substitutes in Modern Thai: A Study in Pronominality. 1969. 70 pp.
    Gld. 21.—
66. MARIA TSIAPERA: A Descriptive Analysis of Cypriot Maronite Arabic: 1969. 69. pp. Gld. 20.—
70. BRENT BERLIN: Tzeltal Numeral Classifiers: A Study in Ethnographic Semantics. 1968. 243 pp.,
    18 plates. Gld. 72.—
71. ROBERT D. STEVICK: Suprasegmentals, Meter, and the Manuscript of "Beowulf". 1968. 88 pp. Gld. 27.—
73. AERT H. KUIPERS: 1. The Squamish Language: Grammar Texts, Dictionary. 1967. 470 pp., map.
    Gld. 110.—
    AERT H. KUIPERS: 2. The Shamish Language: Grammar, Texts, Dictionary. 1969. 98 pp.,
    1 photograph Gld. 24.—
74. ROBERT ALLEN PALMATIER: A Descriptive Syntax of the "Ormulum". 1969. 137 pp. Gld. 24.—
75. HELMUT R. PLANT: Syntaktische Studien zu den Monseer Fragmenten: Ein Beitrag zur Beschreibung
    der inneren Form des Althochdeutschen. 1969. 96 pp. Gld. 24.—
76. ALLAN R. KEILER. A Phonological Study of the Indo-European Laryngeals. 1970. 106 pp. Gld. 30.—
77. J. R. RAYFIELD: The Languages of a Bilingual Community. 1970. 118 pp. Gld. 28.—
78. DIANA L. KAO. Structure of the Syllable in Cantonese. 1971. 189 pp., 22 fig., 50 tables. Gld. 54.—
79. HENRY G. SCHOGT: Le système verbal du français contemporain. 1968. 74 pp. Gld. 20.—
80. KAMIL ZVELEBIL: Comparative Dravidian Phonology. 1970. 202 pp. Gld. 54.—
81. DAVID COHEN: Études de linguistique sémitique et arabe. 1970. 178 pp. Gld. 54.—
82. GARY J. PARKER: Ayacucho Quechua Grammar and Dictionary. 1969. 221 pp. Gld. 64.—
83. JAMES W. GAIR: Colloquial Sinhalese Clause Structures. 1970. 164 pp. Gld. 40.—
84. HIKMET I. SEBÜKTEKIN: Turkish—English Contrastive Analysis. 1971. 116 pp. Gld. 30.—
85. ELMAR SEEBOLD Vergleichendes und Etymologisches Wörterbuch der Germanischen Starken Verben.
    1970. 571 pp. Gld. 132.—
86. GENEVIÈVE N'DIAYE. Structure du dialecte basque de Maya. 1970. 249 pp. Gld. 66.—
87. ANNA FUCHS: Morphologie des Verbs im Cahuilla. 1970. 76 pp. Gld. 35.—
91. JAMES E. COPELAND A Stepmatricial Generative Phonology of German. 1971. 105 pp., 1 table.
    Gld. 28.—
93. MARIO SALTARELLI. A Phonology of Italian in a Generative Grammar. 1970. 96 pp. Gld. 24.—
94. VLADIMIR MILTNER Theory of Hindi Syntax: Descriptive, Generative. Transformational. 1970. 72 pp.
    Gld. 28.—
95. D. BARTON JOHNSON. Transformations and their use in the Resolution of Syntatic Homomorphy:
    Prepositional of Constructions in Contemporary Standard Russian. 1971. 192 pp., 21 tables. Gld. 39.—
96. JÓZEF TOMPA: Ungarische Grammatik. 1968. 426 pp. Gld. 90.—
97. RODOLFO JACOBSON: The London Dialect of the Fourteenth Century. A Transformational Analysis in
    Historical Linguistics. 1970. 193 pp. Gld. 48.—
98. A. CAPELL and H. E. HINCH: Maung Grammar Texts and Vocabulary. 1970. 201 pp., 16 charts.
    Gld. 68.—
99. RONALD ANDREW ZIRIN The Phonological Basis of Latin Prosody. 1971. 91 pp. Gld. 25.—
100. Q. I. M. MOK: Contribution a l'étude des catégories morphologiques du genre et du nombre dans le
    français parlé actuel. 1968. 155 pp. Gld. 40.—
101. WILLIAM H. BROWN, JR.: A Syntax of King Alfred's Pastoral Care. 1970. 91 pp. Gld. 18.—
102. GARY DEAN PRIDEAUX: The Syntax of Japanese Honorifics. 1970. 107 pp. Gld. 28.—
103. DAVID L. SHORES: A Descriptive Syntax of the Peterborough Chronicle from 1122 to 1154. 1971. 224
    pp., 30 tables. Gld. 50.—
105. SANDRA SCHARFF BABCOCK: The Syntax of Spanish Reflexive Verbs: The Parameter of the Middle
    Verb. 1970. 96 pp. Gld. 21.—
106. ANDRÉ-MARCEL D'ANS: Le Créole français d'Haïti: Étude des unités d'articulation, d'expansion et de
    communication. 1968. 181 pp. Gld. 54.—
107. STANLEY TSUZAKI: English Influence on Mexican Spanish in Detroit. 1971. 92 pp., 6 tables, 9 maps.
    Gld. 25.—
108. ROGER J. STEINER: Two Centuries of Spanish and English Bilingual Lexicography, 1590—1800. 1970.
    130 pp. Gld. 23.—
109. BOBBY RAY GLOVER: A History of Six Spanish Verbs Meaning "To Take, Seize, Grasp". 1971. 115 pp.
    Gld. 24.—
110. DUONG THANH BINH: A Tagmemic Comparison of English and Vietnamese Sentences. 1971. 232 pp.,
    3 tables Gld. 68.—
111. CHARLES CARLTON: Descriptive Syntax of the Old English Charters. 1970. 200 pp. Gld. 48.—
112. MICHAEL GRADY: Syntax and Semantics of the English Verb. Phrase. 1970. 84 pp. Gld. 14.—
113. ALEXANDER ISAŠENKO HANS-JOACHIM SCHÄDLICH: A Model of Standard German Intonation. 1970.
    66 pp., plate, record. Gld. 21.—
115. ANDRÉ HAUDRICOURT et ALPHONSE JUILLAND: Essai pour une histoire structurale du phonétisme
    français. 2e éd. révisée 1971. 135 pp., 20 cartes, figs. Gld. 25.—
116. SAMUEL N ROSENBERG: Modern French Ce.: The Neuter Pronoun in Adjectival Predication. 1970.
    222 pp. Gld. 36.—
119. CHARLES RALLIDES: The Tense Aspect System of the Spanish Verb. 1971. 66 pp. Gld. 18.—
149. A G. SCIARONE La place de l'adjectif en Italien moderne. 1971. 112 pp. Gld. 30.—